FOR THE
Rest
OF YOUR LIFE

Living out Your Destiny Blueprint

Denise Capra

D1377613

DEDICATION

I would like to acknowledge some key people who are contributors in my life that influenced me along the way.

My dedication of this book go to:

The late Anna Stewart & Bob Hazlett, influential prophetic ministers in my life regarding this very book.

Nancy Thompson & Leslie Williams and an encouraging women from our writer's workshop.

And life teachers and mentors,
Andrew & Jamie Wommack, Dave & Bonnie Duell &
Dr Jim & Brenda Richards

My family of gifted writers,
Nick & Alison Koumalatsos who challenge and convey great support
and encouragement to me personally
and my son Neil, who writes daily with clarity & perception.

CONTENTS

Introduction

For the *REST* of your life...

How can that be accomplished? By living out your divinely assigned destiny blueprint! Simply stated, my purpose is to forever establish your eternal position of righteousness by faith. When you hear, believe, and receive the good news gospel of Jesus Christ, you lay a foundation *for the rest of your life.* (My wordplay on "rest" is deliberate, as you will see...)

Contained within these pages are a collection of key life experiences—shared through simple revelations—that have marked my heart with liberty and freedom. I'm loving life, and friends, and family. I haven't always, but the more I grow in my true connection with a good Father and Friend, the more I'm learning to relax! Yet, I can be intense. I am passionate and driven by the opportunities God gives me. And through wisdom, awareness, and a renewed mind, I'm choosing to allow my destiny to emerge. I love people, and stirring up a fresh vision for myself and others inspires me. Goals and plans motivate me, but I realize now that I can sabotage them all by trying to control them.

I've been blessed in life by the revelation of God's goodness and grace. Through great mentors who have inspired and influenced me, I now have vision and desire to see God's people deeply rooted in the revelation of His love and grace. Encountering God's unconditional love produced a never-turn-back course for me. His keeping power in my life and ministry is reality now. Personal growth has come through Jesus and what He's done for me. Because He's not fault-finding, I've felt free to allow Him to show me things about myself. Personal development and self-acceptance resulted. Yet, awareness of my true identity as a new person in Christ reminds me of the limitless living available—and there's so much more!

I'm also learning more about others, and how all of us need love and acceptance. We can never fulfill and become who we are destined to be without recognizing the great value God truly has for us. He's not just tolerating our existence. He actually enjoys our company. So please know that I'm praying for you to experience a paradigm shift, an epiphany, your own personal "a-ha" moment concerning the depth of God's love and grace as you read these pages and consider the truths presented within them.

God has stirred this book in me for years. I feel like each chapter is a puzzle piece He has brought together through me. The place of rest is where we "cease our own efforts." The paradox is: We must labor to enter into this place of rest (see Hebrews 4). I hope you'll receive a genuine impartation of trust and rest from the Lord, and that the reward will be the fulfillment of your God-given dreams, desires, and calling!

Chapter 1

Hearts

Words, thoughts, and ideas have been stored up inside of me for years on end. Yet now the time has come to put pen to paper and release this book. Truth be told, it's coinciding with several significant happenings in my life. So I wanted to share my heart with you and give you some relevant scriptural insights that have the potential of bringing lasting change to your life!

Like Paul, my prayer for you is…

> **"As you therefore have received Christ Jesus the Lord, so walk in Him, rooted and built up in Him and established in the faith, as you have been taught, abounding in it with thanksgiving" (Colossians 2:6-7).**

My walk with the Lord has been an unfolding journey of experiences and relationships. Getting God's Word applied and working in life is an application of knowledge and believing in Him to bring it to pass. My husband (Dennis) and I didn't make anything happen in events unfolding—we just believe in the One Who can! We had broken-hearted lives and families generationally. But we've learned how to let go of our past and put on who we are in Christ.

As of the time of this writing (late 2019), we have pastored the same church in Kansas City, Missouri, for 25 years, and been in over 50 countries of the world sharing, preaching, teaching good news, and flowing in the Holy Spirit and His gifts. I feel extremely privileged and honored to work with the Lover of my soul—Jesus! We have launched a local Bible training school that went on for 15 years. Many graduates have gone on in ministry to the nations. Even so, we are still always growing and learning in this life of grace and faith!

A Heart to Hear

This past decade has been such a journey of learning to connect to Jesus in my own heart. Did you know that God is a heart God? He truly is. And He speaks to our hearts constantly! That's why we need to continue cultivating, developing, and protecting this internal sensitivity toward Him in our lives.

Hebrews 10:22 says…

"Let us draw near with a true heart in full assurance of faith, having our hearts sprinkled from an evil conscience and our bodies washed with pure water."

Unbelief corrupts our conscience, and makes it become evil. We must guard against unbelief working in our hearts and minds, especially as it pertains to what was already accomplished for us through Jesus' finished work. You and I are the only ones who can do anything about that. We are responsible for our own heart, mind, and conscience.

I pray that you're believing and receiving the main message of this book—for the REST of your life—would be JUST that. For the duration of your life, you would become so settled and established in believing in the accomplishment of Jesus—that the unfolding plan of God would effortlessly manifest out of your RELATIONSHIP with Him. Stated another way: May the rest in your heart cause your divine destiny to spring forth in your life as a fruit of your intimacy with God for the rest of your days!

Radically Changed

You can often look at the bigger picture of a person's life and see some threads that are woven throughout. Ours has been a transformation of heart and mind in the personal growth and development of realizing we are NOT the center—Jesus is. It's so awesome how He accepts us right where we are. The more we trust and yield to Him, the quicker we can move along.

My husband and I came out of extreme family dysfunction. Married at the ages of 19 and 21, we were too young for what we embarked upon. But we relied upon help from God Who then began growing us up. On our very wedding night—to my shock and surprise—Dennis asked if we could pray together. We had never done that before!

Both of us are from divorced families. Our parents were very hard-working people. Basically they were incompatible, too young, and not believers. They didn't know God as Father and Friend. After my mother and stepfather had a radical conversion in the early 1970s (during the time of a Jesus Movement) our home-life shifted and changed. It was out with the Ouija boards and astrology charts, and in with Bible studies and prayer meetings. There were new trips on Sundays and midweek to the local denominational country church. There were choir practices and youth groups. It was a rigorous lifestyle change for me!

I went from being a little city girl, just previously going to weekly Mass in our Catholic education tradition, to a country girl setting. But it wasn't until my teenage rebellion got so bad that my parents embraced a Full-Gospel church and the book of Acts experience. The baptism in the Holy Spirit radically changed my parents, and they became bold witnesses for Jesus! Through this life-impacting encounter of Him and this growing supernatural experience—over the course of many years—a deliverance happened in our family, our lives, and ultimately in my new marriage I love the relationship we can have with Jesus—through the written Word of God, as well as through Holy Spirit's guidance. Since the Bible reveals He was **"the Word became flesh,"** we can trust Him

(John 1:14). However, this necessitates that we place value on the priority of knowing Him through His Word. God's true nature and character is revealed to us through the Scriptures, not by our theological speculations and unfounded ideas about Him. So often life situations go awry and seem to contradict the promises of God being real to us. That's where we need to become aware of our authority as a believer. We must choose not to let personal opinion, or even life experiences, cloud and distort our thinking. We have to give up trying to define life by what has happened to us—whether good or bad. So many of us were without direction, having no real identity until we came to know Christ. He even has ways of taking those wasted days, and recovering and restoring it all.

Who Am I Anyway?

Over the years, the Lord has been so real to us, writing new things on our hearts. Let's stay connected to Him. What do you say? Will you allow your belief system to change according to the Truth, and come into alignment with Who He says He is and who He says you are?

You may be muttering to yourself right now, "Yeah, right! Who am I anyway that He would be mindful of me?"

Well, that sounds a lot like David, who wondered...

> **"Compared to all this cosmic glory, why would you bother with puny, mortal man or be infatuated with Adam's sons? Yet what honor you have given to men, created only a little lower than Elohim, crowned like kings and queens with glory and magnificence. You have delegated to them mastery over all you have made, making everything subservient to their authority, placing earth itself under the feet of your image- bearers. All the created order and every living thing of the earth, sky, and sea—the**

wildest beasts and all the sea creatures—everything is in submission to *Adam's sons*" (Psalm 8:4-8 TPT).

God has restored our dignity and worth from shame, neglect, and fear of man!

Aggressively Thankful

Over the decades, God has influenced me to be aggressively thankful. I've learned how to thrive in operating thanksgiving by faith.

Trusting the Lord is never complete without genuine gratitude. As we get to know God, and His true nature, we develop a growing appreciation for everything He's done. We become expectant of everything He's going to do in our life and in the generations to come. Even if something bad happens, we can be fully convinced that God had nothing to do with it, nor does He approve of it. Our response is key! We can resist the enemy, and he will flee from us (see James 4:7). We just have to stop believing the lie that says, "God authorizes everything that happens on this fallen planet." No, that's not true! Stuff happens. God is good and the devil is bad (see John 10:10 & James 1:17). Don't confuse the two! Choosing a grateful attitude helps turn everything around.

Another foundational key is to properly distinguish between the two covenants, and which one we as believers in Jesus Christ are in. Just in case you're not sure, let me help you. It's the New Covenant—the one with better promises and a clear revelation of God being a good Father with Jesus as His exact representation (see Hebrews chapters 1 & 8). This makes for a healthy belief system! Yet, the enemy of our souls would like to do nothing more than to confuse and undermine our trust in the goodness of God.

Imagine if you believed to receive a million dollars, you had a windfall, and then your answer came. What would be your response? Wouldn't it be some form of thanksgiving? I'm sure you'd plan on a shopping spree or something radical! However, it's impossible to see the answer to your prayers without some praise to God being expressed. That's because thanksgiving is a vital part of faith—and faith isn't complete without it.

Think about it: Faith without praise is incomplete. When we attempt to trust in God, but are void of praise and thanksgiving before the time we see what we have trusted Him for, then be aware that we are operating in an inferior faith. As we thank the Lord in advance by faith, our faith will abound and reach its highest level.

Stumbling Blocks

As human beings, we often swing, like a pendulum, from one extreme to another. Before Christ (in our "BC days"), Dennis and I partied hard. This later became a factor in our own radical shift. Our backgrounds were full of dysfunction, disorder, and rebellion against the status quo. Then we came into the kingdom of God with radical life transformation!

As newlyweds with a baby on the way and new in the things of the Spirit, we were extremely dogmatic in our vantage point. All of our efforts and endeavors having to do with godly practices were self-imposed disciplines at that time. The reason for changing the way we lived was more out of an obligation mindset. We chose to go to church twice each Sunday (morning & evening) and then a home cell group in the middle of the week. Some of it was very good, and I'm genuinely thankful for our church during that season. We were "sold-out" in our enthusiasm and dedication to God. Much of it was a necessary beginning in our marriage. With our new way of family life, we were trying to break free from old lifestyle patterns. But much of it was also works-based, striving and performance, trying to please God. We were operating out of human self-effort. While commendable, it was a setup for burnout.

You may be wondering, "Oh, so do you think you can live any way you want to and it's just okay?" Of course not! We realized that our way of life was so destructive, and we would never have escaped it had we not adopted some new ways of living to counter those old bad habits. The disciplines gave us a framework for digging some roots down into knowing God's Word, but it was according to the letter, not the Spirit (see Romans 7:6 & 2 Corinthians 3:5-6). The downside was the self-inflicted restraints and limitations that we placed upon ourselves and others. Too much self-effort! Unknowingly, we judged God and ourselves through that belief system, determining what we would even allow ourselves to receive and experience. With that belief system, we were our very own stumbling blocks—limiting and hindering ourselves from experiencing the freedom God had already purchased and wanted for us.

God-Dependent or Self-Sufficient?

As a young believer at a critical juncture of life choices, key insight came to me through looking more closely into the Gospels, and especially the Parable of the Sower (see Mark chapter 4). In fact, more revelation and understanding opened up to me through these Scriptures than I had received in my whole believing journey up until then! Concerning this specific parable, Jesus even said that in understanding it, you would then be able to understand all of the other parables and have a doorway into comprehending how God's kingdom works. I encourage you to read it over for yourself. Reflect on it, ponder it, and meditate on it!

In verses 15-17, Jesus described and interpreted what happens when the Word is sown into hard hearts…

> **"When they hear** [without understanding], **Satan comes immediately and takes away the word that was sown in their hearts. These likewise are the ones sown on stony ground who, when they hear the word, immediately receive it with gladness; and they have no root in themselves, and so endure only for a time. Afterward, when**

tribulation or persecution arises for the word's sake, immediately they stumble" ["are offended" KJV] (Mark 4:15-17, brackets mine).

This gives us clear insight into exactly what is happening in our hearts with how the Word gets planted—or NOT! Jesus even revealed how the enemy is just after the Word, so it won't grow a root system inside of us. But we get to choose. We can meditate the Word and see that seed planted, established, and bear fruit—if we protect it, water it, and don't get offended!

Thank God for softened and open hearts! Heart conditions truly matter. In fact, the condition of the soil of our heart is key! Everything in God's kingdom hinges on our attitude of heart in receiving from the truth of the Word and Jesus being the center of our life.

Psalm 37:4 says...

"Delight yourself also in the LORD, and He shall give you the desires of your heart."

God is so good, so loving, and so desirous for us to fulfill our destiny and purpose. If our hearts can stay pliable, and our minds renewed to the truth, then we will increase our capacity to receive the goodness of God! And I believe He intends it for this life, right here in what the Bible calls **"the land of the living"** (Psalm 27:13).

All too often people want to simply project things off into heaven. Of course, that will be the ultimate fulfillment of our receiving from God and restoration. However, He wants as much as possible of what He paid dearly to provide manifesting on the earth in the here and now through each one of us as believers (see Matthew 6:9-10). It all comes down to this issue of trusting and believing that God wants to be good to us, and that He's big enough to get us where we need to be, if we will stay open to Him.

One of humility's dominant characteristics is a God-dependency and not a self-sufficiency.

You Are the Gardener

In this book, I want to express some of the truths that we have come to cherish deeply out of the treasures within our hearts. Paul wrote in Colossians 2:3 that in Christ...

"...Are hidden all the treasures of wisdom and knowledge."
Whenever we have questions about what we may perceive as an inconsistency in the written Word, we need to look at it through the lens of Jesus being the Source of all wisdom and knowledge (see also 1 Corinthians 1:30). When we look back at the Old Testament, we can glean perception factoring in Jesus as 'our Treasure.' Paul even prayed for believers that our hearts would be encouraged and knit together in love (see Colossians 2:2). He conveyed that we should have a full assurance of understanding to the knowledge of the mystery of God...

"In *WHOM* are hidden all the treasures of wisdom and knowledge"
(Colossians 2:3, emphasis mine).

Did you see that? It's a Person! (A Who is a Person.) And it's a treasure hunt! You can predetermine to stay childlike. You know you have fallen into religion when it's all duty and you are not having fun with God.

The Lord wants your relationship with Him to be worry-free and light...

"Are you weary, carrying a heavy burden? Then come to me. I will refresh your life, for I am your oasis" (Matthew 11:28 TPT).

As I started this journey as a new creation, I was just beginning to find out who I was.

It takes time to know others, and it takes time to know yourself. But remember, your heart condition (the soil) is the key to the fruit from your life. As the good seed of God's Word is sown into your heart, believing prayer is the water.

You are the gardener of your own heart. Give the seed a good place to grow weed-free, and it will flourish and produce much godly fruit (see John 15:16 & Galatians 5:22-23).

God is a Heart-God!

Chapter 2
Women in Wardrobe

In sharing the story of coming out of our mess, in no way do I wish to glorify the nonsense, but rather the overcoming ability of God at work in someone who recognizes their need for a Savior! Our life testimony and message revolves around coming completely to the END of ourselves...

Growing up in divorced families with such self-destructive living—including abuse of drugs and alcohol—we knew we NEEDED Jesus! Our churchgoing and religious endeavors could never make up for all of our rebellion, addictions, chaos, and crises that surrounded us like the dirt cloud around Pigpen (the character from Peanuts). I'd always been a party girl, and I loved people. I usually saw the best in folks and often fell right in the trap of trusting people that I had no business trusting.

This new revelation of me receiving a free gift of righteousness has made more of an impact on my life than any other! Because of knowing and experiencing this truth, I realize I am forgiven, blessed, and qualified already for every promise in the Scriptures. I am good with God, and He's good with me. I am not competing or comparing myself with anyone else. I'm free from fear, guilt, condemnation, and regret! This has only come out of an experience with Jesus and an encounter with His love, then renewing my mind with the truth of His Word. This is one of the most empowering revelations ever. It's energizing!

I love following the thread of this truth through the Word that New Covenant believers—you and I—have been made the righteousness of God in Christ Jesus! (see 2 Corinthians 5:21)

What Are You Wearing?

Knowing my right-standing with God—my righteousness through Christ—in my heart and mind has done more to transform everything else around me than anything else I've ever learned. When I got myself out of the center and realized Jesus was the Center, my soul began to be free to fulfill the internal blueprint God had for me. Investing in my own heart through a lifelong friendship of knowing Jesus as Lord has led me to discover His calling and plan. Now I want to share the simplicity of this truth with everyone I meet. It's not me, but Him—Jesus—living through me! It's His ability to live out the destiny God has had for me from all the way back to my very conception by my parents.

Talk about a great redemptive work! Because my parents conceived me out of wedlock, they decided to get an abortion. This was in the 1960s, so it wasn't yet as common. As they met with an abortion doctor, he looked at my Dad, and then my Mom, and said, "You don't want her to go through that." Can you believe it? I was delivered by divine intervention through an abortion doctor speaking up for me. Now that's supernatural!

Linen Clothing

Linen is spoken of much throughout the Word. John the Revelator defines it simply as **"the righteousness of saints"** (Revelation 19:8 KJV). We know it is a gift (see Romans 5:17). What then would be the greatest benefit to us when we wear it? Well, when we have high—hot—temperatures, the linen keeps us cool. Wow! Meditate on this for a moment and glean from this life-changing truth. Think, "No sweat!"

In the book of Revelation, John depicts what He saw in his prophetic vision on the Isle of Patmos. In chapter 4, he heard a voice saying...

> **"Come up here, and I will show you things which must take place after this"** (Revelation 4:1)

Later, in chapter 19, he wrote...

> **"Let us be glad and rejoice, and give honour to him: for the marriage of the Lamb is come, and his wife hath made herself ready. And to her was granted that she should be arrayed in fine linen, clean and white: for the fine linen is the righteousness of saints"** (Revelation 19:7-8 KJV).

Then again, in the Old Testament book of Ezekiel when the directives for the high priest's specialty clothing are given, the sons of Zadok were told...

> **"They shall have linen bonnets** [turbans] **upon their heads, and shall have linen breeches upon their loins; they shall not gird themselves with anything that causeth sweat"** (Ezekiel 44:18 KJV, brackets mine).

Why the linen turbans in Scripture? To keep our heads cool from overheating. It represents the covering of our minds. I'm talking about an inward rest from stress!

What was the very first area that Jesus redeemed us from? Well, let's consider the Garden of Gethsemane...

> **"And being <u>in agony</u>, He prayed more earnestly. Then His sweat became like great drops of blood falling down to the ground"** (Luke 22:44, emphasis mine).

Doctors tell us that it is possible for the capillary blood vessels that feed the sweat glands to rupture when one is under conditions of extreme physical or emotional stress, causing them to exude blood. This condition is known as hematohidrosis (HE-MA-TOE-HY- DROSIS).

Why is this so significant? In Hebrew, **the word for sweat is ze'ah**. The **root word** of ze'ah is zuwa,' meaning "to tremble, quiver, quake, be in terror," or **"to agitate (as with fear),"** or **"vex."** In other words, sweat involves agitation and being vexed.

This is all symbolic and is a "type" for us in the New Covenant. The reference to a "type" means a foreshadowing of something from the Old Testament revealing something about Jesus in the New Covenant. God loves to use visual aids to illustrate inward truth!

We don't have to sweat it because Jesus has done the work for us. What a paradox! We will be activated to accomplish the impossible without striving and performance. This practical application for me progressively removed layers of religious wet blankets from off of my life. A brand-new person emerged.

When we realize that we are clothed with a garment by our risen King, our pride and self-sufficiency diminishes. We step out of the rut of having our attention fixed on self, getting out of the introspection focused on our own abilities and limitations. Once we really "get it" that we are righteous, we won't have to compete with anyone spiritually (which often happens subconsciously). We are loved and accepted by God—He has created us righteous and holy in His sight! (see Ephesians 4:24)

This means we don't have to put anyone else down to feel better about ourselves. We don't have to slander, malign, or make digs at someone else to feel good about ourselves. Sometimes we are blind to our own self-righteous attitudes, but trust me, others aren't!

Robe of Righteousness

In the Old Testament, Isaiah prophesied and foretold this about our "Robe of Righteousness"...

"I will greatly rejoice in the LORD, my soul shall be joyful in my God; for he hath clothed me with the garments of salvation, he hath covered me with the robe of righteousness, as a bridegroom decketh himself with ornaments, and as a bride adorneth herself with her jewels" (Isaiah 61:10 KJV).

As I mentioned before, this revelation of God's righteousness being given to us as a gift has been the absolute foundation of our walk with the Lord. Once we understood it, we were empowered to blossom into our destiny. Everything God has put on our hearts through desire has come to pass. We are equipped and qualified for every promise. I believe as you meditate on this, you too will be released into walking by faith and seeing dreams and desires fulfilled!

We have seen financial supply meet us right where we were, and then enable us to "GO" and preach the gospel in other places. God has given us divine connections over and over again. His prosperity is His supply to enable us—you and me—to do what we could not do on our own.

Understanding righteousness has been the demarcation point of our life. Being empowered by the Spirit and knowing our right standing in Christ has catapulted us into destiny. I think that's one of the reasons why the enemy of our souls works so much on our thinking. Old mindsets limit us with negative self-talk. Religious wet blankets are allowed to smother us and make us feel like we're never worthy enough to step out into what God has for us. Your destiny is what's on the line!

Follow along with me as I lay out this scriptural journey into seeing God's heart for you to experience freedom in this prophetic picture unveiled. It's time for the women in the wardrobe.

Isaiah 64:6 graphically exposes our need...

"But we are all as an unclean thing, and all our righteousnesses are as filthy rags; and we all do fade as a leaf; and our iniquities, like the wind, have taken us away" (KJV).

What are our own righteousnesses? Notice that this verse didn't say all our "unrighteousness" is as filthy rags. This is saying that all our **"righteousnesses"**, our goodness, is as filthy rags. According to Strong's, the Hebrew word "ED," which was translated **"filthy"** in this verse, means the menstrual cycle. This is saying that in God's sight all our great works—our self-righteousness—are as a dirty menstrual cloth. All that we do on our own to obtain right standing with the Lord is grossly inadequate!

But when we come to Jesus and receive His salvation, we are given His righteousness (2 Corinthians 5:21). So, for us believers, it would be incorrect to say that all our righteousness is as filthy rags. Jesus has become our righteousness, and He's not a filthy rag. Please pardon the graphic depiction—but it's not mine! This is straight out of the Bible. I'm not an old sinner, saved by grace. I WAS an old sinner, but I've been saved by grace. Therefore, I am now the righteousness of God in my born-again spirit (Ephesians 4:24). Because of Jesus, I am not just in the flesh—I am in the Spirit. I am in Christ! (see Andrew Wommack's Living Commentary note on Isaiah 64:6)

The Church – The Woman

As different ministry leaders point out, the Church is often typified as a woman in scripture. So many truths in God's Word are expressed through stories and symbolism.

Notice what the prophet Isaiah declared…

"But we are all as an unclean thing, and all our righteousnesses are as filthy rags" (Isaiah 64:6 KJV).

Can you see it yet? Sin wasn't the main problem. Even from the Old Testament, we see that our self-effort and performance are not what God is after. Our choices are important, and what we are going to believe and put our trust in is important. Our general mode of operation has been behavior modification to prove ourselves righteous and holy. It's a total misrepresentation of the truth to present the gospel that way. Our current ineffectiveness in the body of Christ in reaching the world has to do with us putting trust in ourselves. Doesn't this cause us to separate from the very ones God wants to reach?

As believers in Jesus, we have been clothed with righteousness in Christ...

"He has clothed me with the garments of salvation, He has covered me with the robe of righteousness" (Isaiah 61:10).

The prophet was proclaiming what was to come in Christ. Do you have this robe? If you believe in the simplicity of this good news and receive it, you're wearing it right now!

The Number 12 & the Women

As we look together at these "women," we'll discover a beautiful thread of truth that has come down through the ages to us today. By investigating these New Testament accounts of two specific healings in the book of Mark, we'll see the symbolic and prophetic picture of the Church's restoration to a truth that will bring liberty and revelation through its fulfillment in our day.

The body of Christ has been on a journey through time in this church age. In these last days we are experiencing a restoration of the simple revelation of God's enabling and empowering grace apart from our performance. We are believing for God's demonstration and power to be revealed to a crying and dying world—but that will come through you!

Notice in the passage below the scope of both the older and younger generations. There's a fulfillment of a prophetic picture here. It's all about destiny!

"Now when Jesus had crossed over again by boat to the other side, a great multitude gathered to Him; and He was by the sea. And behold, one of the rulers of the synagogue came, Jairus by name. And when he saw Him, he fell at His feet and begged Him earnestly, saying, 'My little daughter lies at the point of death.

19

Come and lay Your hands on her, that she may be healed, and she will live.' So *Jesus* went with him, and a great multitude followed Him and thronged Him. Now a certain woman had a flow of blood for twelve years, and had suffered many things from many physicians. She had spent all that she had and was no better, but rather grew worse" (Mark 5:21-26).

Old and Young

These two stories are forever linked! Let's pay close attention to the connection. A girl restored to life and a woman healed—these two women typify the Church. One is young and dead, the other is older and dying.

The older woman bleeding and not being fruitful is a picture of much of the Church. We have a problem with reproduction, or harvest. We've felt ineffective, and experienced little or no results. The Church is bleeding. Why? Because of self-righteousness—not individual sin acts. The prophet showed the "**filthy rags**" are "**self-righteousness**" (Isaiah 64:6). That's the issue with the women bleeding in Mark chapter 5. The unfruitfulness is due to the self-righteousness!

The world needs a Savior, not more religious trappings and strivings to prove who we are. Our true identity comes forth by believing who God says we are.

Twelve, the age of the young woman, is key in this chapter too. It represents the 'governmental foundation' and God's authority. The context of the story and the miracle in Mark 5 depicts the woman touching the hem of Jesus' garment with the assurance of receiving healing and restoration. Jesus knew immediately that power was released and He said to her...

"**Daughter, your faith has made you well. Go in peace, and be healed of your affliction**'" (Mark 5:34).

Literally, this can be translated "GO INTO PEACE and be healed." Stop a moment, and let that sink in. Wow!

"While He was still speaking, *some* came from the ruler of the synagogue's *house* who said, 'Your daughter is dead. Why trouble the Teacher any further?'" (Mark 5:35).

One miracle was interrupted by the other!

"As soon as Jesus heard the word that was spoken, He said to the ruler of the synagogue, 'Do not be afraid; only believe'" (Mark 5:36).

He then told them...

"'The child is not dead, but sleeping.' And they ridiculed Him. But when He had put them all outside...Then He took the child by the hand, and said to her, "Talitha, cumi," which is translated, "Little girl, I say to you, arise." Immediately the girl arose and walked, for she was twelve years *of age.* And they were overcome with great amazement" (Mark 5:39-42).

Symbolism

This picture expresses the reality that until we are RESTORED and believe the truth about our righteousness, we will not see the youth (younger—next generation) rise from dead religion.

The daughter of Jairus was twelve years old. This older woman had suffered for twelve years. Jesus touched the girl. The woman touched Jesus. These two intertwining miracles speak of Jesus healing the Gentiles and raising Israel back to life. On His way to raise the Jewish girl, our Lord stopped to heal the Gentile woman. That's what is happening today with Jews and non-Jews.

As the Church (the older woman) is healed and restored with a new assurance in Christ, we'll then see new life arouse righteousness in the next generation (the younger woman) to fulfill purpose and destiny. Hallelujah! This speaks volumes to me of where we are in the last days with the harvest right in front of us. We are women in wardrobe—and the wardrobe is a Robe of Righteousness!

"The Lord gives the command [to take Canaan]; the women who proclaim the good news are a great host (army); the kings of the [enemies'] armies flee, they flee, and the beautiful woman who remains at home divides the spoil [left behind]" (Psalm 68:11-12 AMP).

It's time for us to fully understand the light of this truth! I believe it's a sign of the times.

This speaks to all of us, and especially us women. It's time to rise up and be the catalyst for a gospel revolution! We have freedom in Christ. At a time where there is more oppression, slavery and trafficking happening to women and children, and religious bondage trying to ensnare, not only are we the voice of freedom—but the resurrection life of God is flowing from us into our next generation to bring forth the greatest release of God's love and power ever yet seen!

Chapter 3
Secrets

"He did this in order to fulfill the prophecy: I will speak to you in allegories. I will reveal secrets that have been concealed since before the foundation of the world" (Matthew 13:35 TPT, emphasis mine).

One thing to remember about secrets: There are different motives and intents behind who is doing the sharing. If it's an emotionally healthy person, and that one entrusts us with a secret, we can realize that they may be investing something precious and valuable with us. In the case of the Lord, it's clear He wants to enrich our lives with His secrets revealed. We can entrust Him with all of ours. The enemy's secrets are spread in the dark, shrouded in lies and distortion, intent on undermining trust. God's secrets are revealed in light with the intention of bearing truth, freedom, and release.

"The secret *things belong* to the LORD our God, but those *things which are* revealed *belong* to us and to our children forever" (Deuteronomy 29:29).

God not only wants illumination for us, but also for our children after us!

Family Plan

As most good parents would affirm, usually their most favorite people in their lives are their very own children. Like other good parents, among their highest hopes would be for them to do well in life. You want your kids to be happy!

Through a life of extreme ups and downs, this has unfolded for my adult children in a very roundabout way. Both my son and my daughter—I have one of each—went through a lot of pain as a result of some of their own choices. But they have overcome because of God's hand upon their lives and their revelation of His love for them. The Lord has brought things around relationally and circumstantially, and has completely restored them both. They've turned out to be some of my most favorite people. I genuinely admire them. They're filled with passion and purpose. I respect their hard work ethic and their unique personalities. God's goodness is multiplying to them. Those secrets the Holy Spirit whispered to me early in their childhood have now come to pass.

God spoke to me a clear directive for one of them from John chapter 9 during an impacting time in my life. As I read the story of miraculous healing contained there one day, a very specific word kept jumping out at me…"WASH." Jesus told the blind man to go "WASH." This word stood out to me so much that I even wrote it down in my journal and dated it. Then—just two weeks later—our eight-year-old son got very sick.

We had been on a float trip on the Missouri river that weekend. While driving home our son (Neil) became very sick. He remained in that condition for over 24 hours before we took him to the emergency room. He told us he felt like he was floating. That was scary! While there, the immediate diagnosis was to do surgery. The doctor said, "Yeah, we need to open him up."

Say what? We were in complete disbelief that he was so sick. We thought it was just the flu. Then, in a succession of comments, the Doc said, "I think he may have a ruptured appendix. We need to go in there and WASH him out. Yeah, we need to open him up and WASH that out."

All of a sudden, it triggered my memory! Just two weeks prior, the Holy Spirit had quickened that very word "wash" to me. Then I knew God was trying to prepare me previously for what was happening right in that crisis moment. This brought a huge relief to me that God knew our situation.

He even spoke to us again during the surgery, this time from John chapter 11. He told us, "This sickness will not end in death" (see verse 4). All of our relatives thought we were in denial because we were so peaceful during such a dangerous procedure. God brought us through this by speaking to us from His Word. He revealed His secret to me.

In the Gospel of John, we read that God desires to reveal hidden things to us. He is our Father and Friend. He wants to show us things to come in our lives (see John 16:13). So we can glean insight by looking at some of these secrets revealed through the lives of Old Testament kings, priests, and prophets. Jesus Christ—and what He would be accomplishing for all of us through His life, death, and resurrection—was all foreshadowed. Now He wants to live His divine life through us!

Jesus taught a lot in parables, which are simple stories illustrating spiritual truths. A parable is like a window that allows us to see something that's been there all along, but the perceptive are drawn into it and the reader seeks more understanding, asking, "What's under the surface here?" Many scriptures have a double reference, revealing prophetic insights and clues to deeper meaning. There's such a depth of revelation into God's love. His plan and purpose are unveiled through these simple, meaning-packed stories.

Secret Doors of Opportunity & Influence

Have you ever toured an old mansion? Compared to Europe or the Middle East, there aren't so many old ones here in America. But I have seen some in New England and the Southern United States. It's always an unforgettable experience. I love seeing the furnishings and reminiscing how it may have been back then. Everybody wants to know where the secret door is! And there's usually a hidden button or lever that opens it up. The amazing thing about God is: He is the Door. He wants us to open up and walk right in.

Through His threshold, we enter into so much more. It's a wide open space! Let's go on in to what He has in store for our lives in Him. Maybe we aren't expecting to find it, but He wants to be good to us. If we pay attention and stay sensitive to His leading, we'll walk right through an opening that brings us into a place of connection, opportunity, and influence. God has His ways of setting us up with divine meetings at the right time with the right people. We just have to show up! Go ahead, ask the Lord to help you be at the right place and right on time!

This has happened to me many times. Secret desires of mine came to pass. I couldn't even quite articulate it, but God knew. My heavenly Father paid attention. He wants to surprise us with the fulfillment of those very things. Those deep desires and dreams started unfolding when my restored soul could begin to receive them—desires to teach and see families restored, to travel and experience other cultures and nations.

Losing Daddy, Gaining a Father

As a young girl, I had been raised by a single mother. I only knew lack and loss. Although my grandparents were loving and affirming, I still experienced much disappointment. Around age 7, my mother re-married and moved us away from the security of our loving grandmother—who took care of us daily—to a new life in a new school, new state, and new family. It wasn't at all what my Mom and Stepdad expected it to be!

Then my Father died. He was too young- only 37. I was 12. It happened just after Christmas, while we were visiting St. Louis during our winter break. He passed suddenly and unexpectedly. I was looking forward to riding back home to Kansas City with him, but right before New Year's Day, he suffered a massive heart attack and was gone.

Without the knowledge of a Savior, there was a hopeless sinking sadness that surrounded me. With so much broken-heartedness while so young, there was no way to express it except for tears and turning the pain inside. I didn't know how to process the engulfing mourning and sadness, so it became an abiding emotion. Only God can take the grief, sorrow, and disillusionment and bring release.

Within just a year, I came to Christ in a country church. The release from the secret pain and trauma began. It started to be erased. By being born again, now the SEED was planted. The new species of being came alive through new birth. Little did I know the seed of greatness (Jesus) that lived within me! Later, a blossoming would come forth over time through this union with Christ.

Today I'm looking forward and smiling at the future!

New Revelation from God's Word

"Having made known unto us the <u>mystery of his will</u>, according to his good pleasure which he hath purposed in himself: that in the dispensation of the fullness of times he might gather together in one all things in Christ, both which are in heaven, and which are on earth; even in him" (Ephesians 1:9-10 KJV, emphasis mine).

Compare this same passage in *The Passion Translation*, which says…

"And through the revelation of the Anointed One, he unveiled his secret desires to us—the hidden mystery of his long-range plan, which he was delighted to implement from the very beginning of time. And because of God's unfailing purpose, this detailed plan will reign supreme through every period of time until the fulfillment of all the ages finally reaches its climax—when God makes all things new in all of heaven and earth through Jesus Christ" (Ephesians 1:9-10 TPT).

Now that's music to my ears—to know a personal God Who actually has a long range plan!

Bible scholar A.T. Robertson points out that the Greek word **"MUSTERION,"** translated **"mystery"** here, means *"something that could not be known by men except by divine revelation, but that, though once hidden, has now been revealed in Christ and is to be proclaimed so that all who have ears may hear it."* This truth applies to each of us personally, and flows through us to others.

When I first began truly understanding how the kingdom of God operated, I immediately encountered opposition. I had already been a believer for over ten years, but for the first time I was gaining new perception. Everything around me was trying to choke out or steal understanding—in a big way. I felt like I was in the Twilight Zone! One way this occurred was through persecution for the Word's sake (see Mark 4:17). People who I believed were my friends were silently rejecting me and cutting me off. Everything had been great in our church experience up until that time, but now they seemed so perplexed by us. Some were even actually falsely accusing us. We were just excited about the new things we were seeing in God's Word!

I was shocked, and wondered, *How could this be happening to us?* Then the truth in Mark 4:17 started opening up to me…

> **"For when trouble or persecution comes on account of the Word, they immediately wilt and fall away"** (TPT).

The goal of the enemy is to keep the seed of God's Word from taking root in a believing heart because of the threat we are to him through bearing fruit in the kingdom of God. My husband and I began witnessing some healing miracles by taking hold of God's promises by faith. Then stuff happened! But once I knew this tactic of the enemy—that trouble or persecution comes on account of the Word—it diffused and disempowered the strategy of darkness. I could choose to NOT give up the seed of God's promises. This simple revelation explained so much to me. We had gone from a positive rapport with everyone to a completely unwarranted invisible animosity. How could we understand what was happening? Well, by reading and meditating on this parable of the sower sowing the seed in Mark chapter 4 and Matthew chapter 13.

Once I understood how Gods Word operates in a believer, it was really impossible to steal because this truth was germinating in my heart. This secret—this mystery revealed—was valuable treasure containing inherent power within. Once believed upon, it released exponential power to transform people and circumstances. Then in actuality, effortless change began to take place! The only 'labor' came in the form of renewing my mind to the truth of His love, grace, and forgiveness. Fruit began to flourish in our lives and started to affect many other people as well. It was now being multiplied. Despite some divided relationships, which we had nothing to do with, lives were changed. Some people began to experience freedom and miracles. We were more stable and confident, witnessing transformation in lives all around us—including our own.

I remember standing in faith with a family whose teenage son had been given a horrible diagnosis after reacting to a drug. Because the parents knew their authority in Christ, we all stood in faith together and saw him—against all the odds—come out of a coma. The doctors said he would never come out, but remain in a vegetative state for the rest of his life. We spoke over him in faith and called him out of that coma, speaking to his body and to his brain with faith in God's promises. Within a few weeks, he came out of that coma! They said he'd never walk again. Well, he walked out of the hospital in a short time.

Union with Christ

I love reading Paul's letters. They contain some of the most wonderful revelations about the believer's union with Christ found anywhere in Scripture. He prayed…

> **"Because of this, since I first heard about your strong faith in the Lord Jesus Christ and your tender love toward all his devoted ones, my heart is always full and overflowing with thanks to God for you**

29

as I constantly remember you in my prayers. I pray that the Father of glory, the God of our Lord Jesus Christ, would impart to you the riches of the Spirit of wisdom and the Spirit of revelation to know him through your deepening intimacy with him. I pray that the light of God will illuminate the eyes of your imagination, flooding you with light, until you experience the full revelation of the hope of his calling—that is, the wealth of God's glorious inheritances that he finds in us, his holy ones!"** (Ephesians 1:15-18 TPT).

You are the treasure chest.

And again from a couple of chapters later…

"So I kneel humbly in awe before the Father of our Lord Jesus, the Messiah, the perfect Father of every father and child in heaven and on the earth. And I pray that he would unveil within you the unlimited riches of his glory and favor until supernatural strength floods your innermost being with his divine might and explosive power. Then, by constantly using your faith, the life of Christ will be released deep inside you, and the resting place of his love will become the very source and root of your life" (Ephesians 3:14-17 TPT).

Paul wrote this from prison. During his darkest moments, he shared his prayer life with us and for us—with secrets waiting to be unveiled therein.

Mysteries Revealed

Now we know. After all the suspense, to me, this was my marching orders!

"For this wonderful mystery, which I briefly described, was given to me by divine revelation, so that whenever you read it you will be able to understand my revelation and insight into the secret mystery of the Messiah. <u>There has never been a generation that has been given the detailed understanding of this glorious and</u>

divine mystery until now. He kept it a secret until this generation. God is revealing it only now to his sacred apostles and prophets by the Holy Spirit. Here's the secret: **The gospel of grace has made you, non-Jewish believers, into coheirs of his promise through your union with him**. And you have now become members of his body—one with the Anointed One!" (Ephesians 3:3-6 TPT)

Wait, what? You mean, never before had this been illuminated? This puts all of us living in the last two thousand years in a unique category. He's trusting us with a revealed secret. The cat is out of the bag!

We usually don't trust someone who can't keep a secret. So, conversely, it's endearing to know that God can keep all of our secrets because of how much He knows us. He's so amazing! Now He reveals His very own secrets with us, counting us as trustworthy and capable of doing something with what He's shown us.

God is so *purpose-driven*, He's intentional. So is Holy Spirit...

"But when the truth-giving Spirit comes, he will unveil the reality of every truth within you. He won't speak his own message, but only what he hears from the Father, and he will reveal prophetically to you what is to come" (John 16:13 TPT).

I love this, and count on it!

Most people enjoy a good drama or mystery story. You may even subscribe to Netflix or something similar. So of course, we are very captivated when we find that Paul speaks of a divine mystery revealed to us. That has made me want to search it out completely, and then go public with it. What an announcement!

Paul shared his goal here...

"My passion is to enlighten every person to this divine mystery. It was hidden for ages past until now, and kept a secret in the heart of God, the Creator of all. **The purpose of this was to unveil before every throne and rank of angelic orders in the heavenly realm God's full and diverse wisdom revealed through the church. This perfectly wise plan was destined**

31

from eternal ages and fulfilled completely in our Lord Jesus Christ, so that now we have boldness through him, and free access as kings before the Father because of our complete confidence in Christ's faithfulness" (Ephesians 3:9-12 TPT).

Multi-faceted & Multi-sided Wisdom

Oh, such insights to glean and apply! The *New King James Version* says...

"To the intent that now the manifold wisdom of God might be made known <u>by the church</u> to the principalities and powers in the heavenly *places*" (Ephesians 3:10).

This is like rubbing the devil's nose in the kingdom of darkness' defeat! We all have something to say. God's many-sided wisdom comes through us, and what we say affects the spiritual order of everything. We have something to think and say to the whole universe. We are God's mouthpiece to all of creation. Did you grasp what Paul was sharing with us? We, as the Church, are now in a position of dispersing and dispensing the wisdom of God to creation and the spiritual realm. That also clearly implies that we must come to know who we are.

Realize that through Christ...

"*For it is not from man that we draw our life* but from God as we are being joined to Jesus, the Anointed One. And now he is our God-given wisdom, our virtue, our holiness, and our redemption" (1 Corinthians 1:30 TPT).

Applying this to everyday life, we can have more confidence and authority in our believing prayers. Did you know that God has deposited in us what is needed for whatever we are facing? It's true! We have supernatural solutions whatever the situation—financial difficulty, health crisis, etc. We may need to know what lies ahead concerning our destiny. We aren't begging for a miracle, but we are rising up to the occasion with a secure place in God to enforce the enemy's defeat, which was accomplished a long time ago at the Cross. We can believe in the win, even before we see it! It's time for real life application at home, at work and everywhere we go.

Ears to Hear & Eyes to See?

When Jesus was asked why He spoke in parables, He answered...
> **"Because it has been given to you to know the mysteries of the kingdom of heaven, but to them it has not been given"** (Matthew 13:11).

He also said...
> **"The measure [of thought and study] you give [to the truth you hear] will be the measure [of virtue and knowledge] that comes back to you—and more [besides] will be given to you *who hear"*** (Mark 4:24 AMPC).

What is hidden from the masses, by their hardness of heart, is made obvious to the soft, pliable heart!

Those who choose to learn about the Kingdom and its operation fall into a very blessed and unique category. This is us! Jesus is our code breaker.
> **"But blessed *are* your eyes for they see, and your ears for they hear; for assuredly, I say to you that many prophets and righteous *men* desired to see what you see, and did not see *it,* and to hear what you hear, and did not hear *it"*** (Matthew 13:16-17).

Wow, what a time to be alive!

Purpose & Appreciation for the Mystery

The mystery spoken of here involves *not only* the Gentiles sharing the promise of the Messiah but also the Jews and Gentiles being joint-heirs with the Messiah and incorporated into His one body...

33

"Here's the secret: The gospel of grace has made you, non-Jewish believers, into coheirs of his promise through your union with him. And you have now become members of his body—one with the Anointed One!" (Ephesians 3:6 TPT).

This is the mystery that was unknown in the Old Testament and revealed in the New Testament to His apostles and prophets by the Spirit. Paul said that through reading his words, the mystery of the Gentiles and Jews being one body could be understood. By reading His Word and the enlightenment of the Holy Spirit that Jesus in His fullness is known. Believers are united *not only* to Christ, but also to each other. The Gentiles did not become part of some Jewish body, but Jew and Gentile became part of the new body of Christ. In context, the mystery Paul spoke of is that the Gentiles are equal heirs with the Jews in the body of Christ.

Did you ever consider the fact that Paul was one of the apostles, but was one that did not actually walk with Jesus? Instead, he knew Him more by his relationship with the Holy Spirit. Paul's apostleship was not bestowed upon him from the earthly Jesus, as was the case with the other apostles. His commission came from the resurrected Lord Jesus Christ (see Acts 9). This means so much to us individually with our relationship to the Holy Spirit. His calling to us is personal. Getting to know Him by His Word through His Spirit is living directives to each of us. I began to experience this direction, guidance, instruction and deeper personal connection.

In Colossians, another letter of his, which is a companion teaching to the book of Ephesians, Paul said the mystery was…

"Christ in you, the hope of glory" (Colossians 1:27).

The particulars of the church were a mystery in the Old Testament. But in the New Testament, every detail of this mystery is intended to be <u>fully revealed</u>—even to demonic powers! God's church is like a city set on a hill for all the world to see (Matthew 5:14). This is God's mandate and call for overflowing, out-flowing love to touch the hurting world, again Christ in us the hope of glory.

In his life and ministry, Paul testified that he was one who received by the revelation of Jesus. As an apostle commissioned, one sent by the Lord, he served as a credentialed messenger, what today we would call an "ambassador." I look at myself as an ambassador for Christ (see 2 Corinthians 5:20). I consider all missionaries to be ambassadors. To the Corinthians, Paul admitted...

> **"When I first came to proclaim to you the secrets of God, I refused to come *as an expert*, trying to impress you with my eloquent speech and lofty wisdom"** (1 Corinthians 2:1 TPT).

He fully relied on God and His spiritual power working in him...

> **"After all, who can really see into a person's heart and know his hidden impulses except for that person's spirit? So it is with God. His thoughts and <u>secrets</u> are only fully understood by his Spirit, the Spirit of God"** (1 Corinthians 2:11 TPT, emphasis mine).

The Secret Is Out!

> **"Don't fool yourself. Don't think that you can be wise merely by being up-to-date with the times. Be God's fool—that's the path to true wisdom. What the world calls smart, God calls stupid. It's written in Scripture, He exposes the chicanery of the chic. The Master sees through the smoke screens of the know-it-alls"** (1 Corinthians 3:19-20 MSG).

What is the so-called wisdom we're being warned about? A cleverness that pretends to solve the meaning of life apart from God—that thinks intelligence supersedes faith and that knowledge itself produces goodness. Well, well, well-this puts things into perspective. We can give up all our authoritative lofty opinions. Instead, we should say, "I submit my imagination to Your revelation and truth." Why settle for a relationship with the "universe" (the recent buzzword to avoid saying God) when the One Who spoke the universe into existence knows you by name and loves you? Why not just relate directly with Him?

Humbly, of course…

> **"I don't want to hear any of you bragging about yourself or anyone else. <u>Everything is already yours as a gift</u>—Paul, Apollos, Peter, the world, life, death, the present, the future—all of it is yours, and you are privileged to be in union with Christ, who is in union with God"** (1 Corinthians 3:21-23 MSG, emphasis mine).

This treasured insight settles my soul to know that I can let down walls of self-protection. God's unique purpose for me is happening. There's no need to prove anything to anyone else—and especially myself. I can be secure in who He has made me to be, enjoying my connection with the Lord and trusting Him in each new day to bring to pass His will. He can stir up His direction for me, and as I yield to Him, I'll walk out His will for me. This will affect marriages, families and work-relationships.

Did you know that angels have long been curious concerning these things?

> **"This salvation was the focus of the prophets who prophesied of this *outpouring of* grace that was destined for you. They made a careful search and investigation of the meaning *of their God-given prophecies* as they probed into *the mysteries* of who would fulfill them and the time period when it would all take place. The Spirit of the Anointed One was in them and was pointing prophetically to the sufferings that Christ was destined to suffer and the glories that would be released afterward. God revealed to the prophets that their ministry was not for their own benefit but for yours. And now, you have heard these things from the evangelists who preached the gospel to you through *the power of* the Holy Spirit sent from heaven—the gospel *containing <u>wonderful</u> <u>mysteries</u>* that even the**

angels long to get a glimpse of" (1 Peter 1:10-12 TPT, emphasis mine).

If this is a mystery that even angels seek to know more about, how much more is waiting for you and me to discover through revelation and relationship with our awesome God! The secret is out. Our journey is on, and we're cooperating!

Chapter 4
Images

We're living in a time when fake news is off the charts! Everyone depicts and promotes a false front. Do you own a selfie-stick? How would you want to be portrayed in advertising and marketing? Do you put up a façade? Have you ever tried to project a false image in order to persuade an audience to buy into whatever you're selling? Personally, I don't like the feeling when it seems like someone is trying to sell me something. Our culture festers these facades as a breeding ground for keeping up appearances!

Do you feel free to be yourself? Our book, *Are You A Dung Beetle: How to Break Free from the Performance Trap*, is just as enlightening now as it was when we first released it more than a decade ago. The truths contained in that book helped us get established in our New Covenant benefits and reminded us of God's love for us. We were set free to be ourselves in Christ.

Because of what the Lord told him...

"My grace is sufficient for you, for My strength is made perfect in weakness"

Paul declared...

"Therefore most gladly I will rather boast in my infirmities, that the power of Christ may rest upon me" (2 Corinthians 12:9).

God was showing Paul, "When you give up, I can take over." Anytime we stop trusting in ourselves, but trust in Him instead, the Lord shows His strength. It's when we lean on our own abilities that we get in trouble.

Paul had more reason to trust in himself than his critics did—he had the better track record. But the apostle learned the lesson of not trusting in himself. In fact, he counted all his accomplishments as manure (or dung; see Philippians 3:7-8), and he became totally dependent upon Christ living through him (see Galatians 2:20). Paul learned to be weak in himself so that Christ could be strong in him.

We can all be who God created us to be when we relax and accept ourselves. He's accepted us. I began my journey in God released from old habits by discovering my new nature in Christ. I am not who I was! God has called us, anointed us, and set us apart for service, but I can never get my identity from my old self or even our new calling in ministry. As His child, it's all about our intimacy and friendship with Him!

My husband and I have had a burning passion to see people get established in the simplicity of the revelation of His love, grace, and goodness. From my perspective, people desire to know the truth, but are afraid to trust and don't want a religious formula. They desire what's real, and want to know someone cares. That rapport often takes time to build, but God in His faithfulness divinely orchestrates life so we can get this message to others. He just needs our willingness, faith, and availability. How sensitive are you to His Spirit's leading?

How do you see yourself? As a young married couple, we had to ask ourselves that question too. Who are we? The Holy Spirit initiated things inside of us and then connected us to things we were passionate about. What moved us into action?

39

Freedom in Oneness

Dennis and I saw ourselves as a team—a husband and wife team. Jesus prayed this prayer for us as the body of Christ…

> **"I do not pray for these alone, but also for those who will believe in Me through their word; that they all may be one, as You, Father, *are* in Me, and I in You; that they also may be one in Us, that the world may believe that You sent Me. And the glory which You gave Me I have given them, that they may be one just as We are one: I in them, and You in Me; that they may be made perfect in one, and that the world may know that You have sent Me, and have loved them as You have loved Me"** (John 17:20-23).

We're speaking of oneness here, just as God is one—Father, Son & Holy Spirit. We need to understand the relationships we need to have to be "one."

> **"But he who is joined to the Lord is one spirit *with Him*"** (1 Corinthians 6:17).

When your marriage is working together, it will represent the Trinity and show what God is doing. The enemy tries to break up the image of God when we are not "one." Even before we were born again, my husband and I genuinely connected together in purpose. We tapped into our gift of hospitality by being people-oriented and relational. We used to throw parties for others and bartended together. After receiving Jesus, we recognized that although our serving attitude had been misplaced, God had put serving people in us as part of our calling in Christ. We began hosting a weekly cell group meeting in our home. Months became years, and years became a decade. What a great way to develop people skills and hospitality to bless, not just impress! Through hosting people regularly, we developed a protective sense regarding them. We cared about how God was being represented to them. The Lord called us to shepherd His flock.

Freedom in the Divine Image

"Then God said, 'Let Us make man in Our image, according to Our likeness; let them have dominion over the fish of the sea, over the birds of the air, and over the cattle, over all the earth and over every creeping thing that creeps on the earth.' So God created man in His *own* image; in the image of God He created him; male and female He created them" (Genesis 1:26-27).

God created man and woman in His image. His image is the Father, Son, and Holy Spirit in unity. He created male and female. God created us to have dominion over the birds, over the fish, over the "creeps," but He did not create us to have dominion over each other. We get into messed up thinking when one thinks they can dominate the other.

It doesn't go very well if I try to dominate. At different times through the years, I've tried to "fix" my spouse, and he's tried to "fix" me. Finally we realized we weren't called to fix each other. Changes don't come about through domination or trying to fix one another. There's a better way than trying to fix a person—submit to God and pray for them. When we turn our relationships over to God, and pray and encourage the other person, somehow a ray of light comes from things other people have been trying to tell us all along through the years, and now the truth sets us free.

Over the course of many years raising a family, we've seen a progressive restoration in our own family. We had misunderstanding and misplaced ideas about God's true nature, and the 'law vs. grace' mentality. Learning how healthy boundaries work has brought new connection and help to our lives. Identity, settled in the love God has for me, allows me to glean from the image of God on the inside of me.

By God investing His divine image in us, He is saying that we are the deputies over and caretakers of the earth. That was the original plan—we were given stewardship over the earth. Like the animals, we were made from dust. However, God breathed His breath into man, and we have the breath of life from God.

What is modeled for us in the Godhead between God the Father, God the Son, and God the Holy Spirit? Equality! *There is no hierarchy in the Trinity.* The hierarchy concept is derived from Greek-type of philosophy. That's another subject too (see the excellent book *Why Not Women?* by Loren Cunningham & David Joel Hamilton with Janice Rogers).

Our creating, redeeming, and empowering God works through fragile, unlikely instruments. Often when we think of the Trinity as family, we see God as top, Jesus the middle, and Holy Spirit as the bottom. Jesus prayed…

> **"Now I am no longer in the world, but these are in the world, and I come to You. Holy Father, keep through Your name those whom You have given Me, that they may be one as We *are*"** (John 17:11).

Throughout the years, the Church as a whole has tried to create a hierarchical system with the "Grand Poohbah" at the top, and the lay people and little people somewhere down the line. God never set it up that way. He set it up for us all to be servants. I am a servant of the Most High God! Even though the ministry call is a high calling, no one is better than someone else. The responsibilities and the position of pastor or elder is a job function describing how someone serves the body of Christ, and it is valued equally in God's eyes. Our image of God, how we see ourselves, and how we see others will affect everything in our lives!

Birth of Religion

Looking back over the scope of history, from the time of Cain & Abel, brothers, in the book of Genesis; people have been trying to impress God with the fruits of *their* labor. And from the time of Cain, God has been rejecting their offerings. Why?

"The LORD looked with favor on Abel and his offering, but on Cain and his offering he did not look with favor" (Genesis 4:4-5 NIV).

As the story goes, Abel offered the firstborn of his flock while Cain brought a fruit basket. Why was Abel's offering accepted while Cain's was not? The Scripture says...

"By faith Abel offered to God a more excellent sacrifice than Cain, through which he obtained witness that he was righteous" (Hebrews 11:4).

Abel's sacrifice revealed what he believed. Cain's did too. Faith is always a response to something God has said or done. So, what was Abel responding to? The sacrificial gift God had given to Adam and Eve in the Garden. Think about this, while Abel's faith was in response to what God had done, Cain's faith was in the work of his own hands, his own effort. Herein lays the very roots of religion!

What clearer picture of man's self-effort could there be than Adam and Eve using fig leaves to cover themselves when they saw they were naked after eating from the tree of the knowledge of good and evil. What did God do? He covered them with animal skins, thus instituting the first blood sacrifice. We must come to the end of self and trust instead in what the Lamb of God—our Lord Jesus Christ—has fully accomplished in His sacrificial death, burial, and resurrection. God's got us covered!

Fast-forward to today. Are we believing what God says, or are we conjuring up our own big ideas? Do we approach God on the basis of the New Covenant and its terms as expressed in Scripture? Or do we come to Him with our own version of how we see it? That's where images are morphed and altered. Do we create God in the image we design?

Abel considered what God had done, but Cain wanted God to look at what he had done. Big mistake! Instead of responding to God in faith, Cain tried to forge his own religion and was rejected.

Dave Duell—a life mentor in ministry—used to always define religion as a "mass of externals to cover up man's own weakness." We can even call it "a return to bondage." It's nothing but man's view of God and man's attempts to appease God on our own terms. We don't create an image of God. He is the "I AM." We gain our image and identity from who He says we are. And the New Covenant is filled with that description in every verse that says, "in Christ," because that's who we are.

I recognize that James 1:27 uses the word "religion" in a positive sense, saying...

> **"Pure and undefiled religion before God and the Father is this: to visit orphans and widows in their trouble, *and* to keep oneself unspotted from the world."**

I'm using this word, "religion," in the bad sense, the sense that it has always valued control as a substitute for viable, relevant ministry and connection. Tradition and culture have always been enemies of the Gospel. They're constantly trying to trap us in lifeless ruts and activities, creating a false sense of security by clinging to methods that are familiar but ineffective. We think they're holy because they were used by the last generation. Tradition is so opposed to the Gospel that Jesus gave this incredible warning...

> **"You have a fine way of setting aside the commands of God in order to observe your own traditions!...Thus you nullify the word of God by your tradition that you have handed down. And you do many things like that"** (Mark 7:9,13 NIV).

Religion projects an image. There are vast amounts of religion in our world. But here, I am contrasting these two brothers, two religions. Religion based on human effort is unacceptable to God. You can toil and bring costly sacrifices every day of your life, but it will not improve your standing before Him one bit. We cannot buy our salvation with humanitarian efforts and philanthropy. You can't buy your way into eternal life!

Neither can we go back in time and make animal sacrifices. The blood of animals does nothing to take away our sins (see Hebrews 10:4). Before the Cross these things only had value because they pointed ahead to the blood of Jesus. We're on the other side of the Cross now. We look back to what was accomplished. The Lamb of God has come, and His one-time sacrifice was more than enough to account for all the sin of the world (see Hebrews 9:26).

It's vital that we let all of this go! In order to really move into your created purpose, you must let go of all the religion, tradition, and false fronts; and adopt who you really are in Christ, which is your true image and identity now that you're born again.

I remember not really knowing who I was early in my Christian life. I tried so hard to be like someone else who I thought was a godly example that I stifled my own personality. I grew to resent the unknowing person because I really couldn't be like them. Ha! What freedom to get to know yourself in Christ—who God created YOU to be—and to like and appreciate that person. Be yourself! Then others can begin to be comfortable with themselves because you are comfortable with yourself and them. It's a freeing way to relate to others, and it allows you to become a safe person.

Identity in Christ

In our growth, settling our identity in Christ produced security for our hearts and lives. It displaced the 'abandonment' issues we had from divorced family living. I remember first understanding 'sonship,' which is our adoption into the family of God as His very own child. He is our Daddy. We discovered the truth that we were no longer slaves, but free and friends with God! This became more real than any leftover supposed rejection issues from childhood. Now in Christ, I began to understand I have a new family identity.

I experienced closeness with those in my local church. This widened my horizon and borders. Of course I valued my biological family, but I really began to see the eternal value in my spiritual family—the body of Christ.

Divine Connections

Back in the early 1990s, we took our first step of faith to go on a mission trip, which was a big stretch for our thinking. We trusted the Lord to provide, launching out to do it, and even preparing to fly across the "pond" (Atlantic Ocean). Within a couple of months, construction work increased at my husband's job, a few people gave gifts to help send us, and we experienced supernatural supply!

That mission trip in 1992 ended up being such a key trip—not only for us, but for many other people too. Divine connections were made and many people were launched forward in ministry from that trip. It also became the first seed of a faith walk that has continued throughout our lifetime ever since!

We've been partners with Andrew Wommack Ministries for decades. God is using him mightily in our time as a Reformer in the body of Christ. During that trip to Andrew's first Grace & Faith Conference in the United Kingdom, God used him in such a strategic way to introduce us to many key people whom we've been associated with ever since. We first met Dave and Bonnie Duell on a tour bus in the UK. They were pastors and apostles operating in gifts of faith and working of miracles, with signs and wonders following. God connected our hearts with theirs to help with a vision they had for a network of ministries. It was a faith and grace based, relational style ministry. I remember specifically asking the Lord on the flight over the pond to the United Kingdom this question: "What is Your purpose for us in this trip?"

Before ever meeting this special couple, God showed me the verse…

"For I long to see you, that I may impart to you some spiritual gift, so that you may be established—that is, that I may be encouraged together with you by the mutual faith both of you and me" (Romans 1:11).

Wow, through this passage from Paul, the Lord spoke to me what was coming. We would be established and strengthened through the connection with one another! We worked with the Duells for over 20 years launching Bible schools, training and hosting leadership conferences in many other countries, and here in the USA. We learned so much about living by faith and trusting in God for His supply to fulfill the vision that He gives. Because of the supernatural gifts working through Dave and Bonnie, we saw great demonstrations from the Holy Spirit. Bonnie's skills in administration helped train me in that area. They had an honoring mutuality in their leadership style, along with a loving gift of hospitality. The way they humbly served others helped lay a great foundation in our lives. God uses people to help disciple others!

Through Andrew Wommack's encouragement, we met another great teacher and mentor, Dr. Jim Richards and his wife Brenda. He actually gave us his audio teachings. No words can describe how meaningful his wisdom, books, and friendship has been to our lives, family, and ministry. Dr. Jim's apostolic teaching has profoundly changed us, and his materials are changing the way the world sees God. To this day we are still experiencing the impact of these dedicated ministers whom we met either on or because of that mission trip.

And we've traveled often ever since! Dennis has been in over 50 countries, many of them multiple times. I've been in over 40 countries, also many of them multiple times. Our passion is to see leadership foundations launched in people's hearts and lives through understanding the finished work of Jesus. We have been so privileged to speak in churches all over the world!

Will you allow God to use you to mentor and disciple others? It's an investment of your life, time, and energy. If you are willing, He will make a way for you!

We are committed to help bring release to people who genuinely have a heart for God but are trapped in lifeless, legalistic religious systems because of 'not rightly dividing the Word' (2 Timothy 2:15).

An insightful Bible teacher, Paul Ellis, who clearly understands the distinctions in the covenant, says, "*Just as there are only two religions, there are two kinds of preacher: Those who say we are qualified by works and those who say we are qualified by the blood of Jesus. These two preachers may look the same, but their messages could not be more different.*"

What you believe inside protects the outside. Have you realized that Jesus gave Himself as the last sacrifice of the Old Covenant? He was offered on the altar of the Cross to defeat Satan. Not only did He become our sin, the blood He shed is for the protection of those who receive it by faith (see 2 Corinthians 5:21). The enemy was defeated completely. Principalities and powers were spoiled in Christ's victory over death!

> **"He canceled out every legal violation we had on our record and the old arrest warrant that stood to indict us. He erased it all—our sins, our stained soul—he deleted it all *and they cannot be retrieved!* Everything we once were in Adam has been placed onto his cross and nailed permanently there as a public display of cancellation"** (Colossians 2:14 TPT).

This "stained soul" has been erased of its filth. The word "erased" explicitly holds the concept of removal of stains. This means the nature of Adam has been removed and the nature of Christ has been embedded into us. We've been totally set free from every trace of sin by the power of the blood of Jesus Christ. No leftovers or things from our past can affect our future, unless we allow it to be a limiting belief through deception
(footnote a in TPT).

The reference to '***Everything we once were in Adam***' in the Aramaic can be translated "***from our midst.***" This would refer to all that was within us—the core of our past life and its memories of failure and disobedience. A new DNA has been embedded now within us through the Cross and resurrection life of Christ (footnote b in TPT).

After the resurrection, Jesus then stepped out of the tomb and told us...

"All authority has been given to Me in heaven and on earth" (Matthew 28:18).

He then gave it to us. We have a new job description: "*Therefore **now you go** into all the world. You take My name, you lay hands on the sick and they'll recover. You cast out the devil. I whipped him; you go enforce it.*" It's the Great Commission, not the great suggestion!

Talk about game changers? This is an IMAGE CHANGER!

As Dr. Jim Richards writes in his *Leadership That Builds People* manual...

"Even Jesus had to grow in wisdom! (to have security within). As Luke said in his gospel, '**And Jesus increased in wisdom and stature, and in favor with God and men**' (Luke 2:52). If He GREW in these things – He didn't have them all. This is how Jesus prepared for living and ministering—by preparing within. He established His heart in His identity according to what He read about Himself in the scriptures. We must be honest with ourselves. None of the truths we believe and teach will consistently work from a heart that is affected by insecurity and rejection.

Up until the time Jesus came on the scene, the Jews had no concept of GOD as Father. "*The Old Testament word for Father was not an intimate word. It was more like the word, 'Master.' Of the more than 200 references to God as Father, less than 20 of them are in the OLD TESTAMENT.*" Our Father determines our identity. In discovering and believing who His Father really was—JESUS found His true identity. We are NOT who we used to be. We are sons by adoption.

This will be our lifetime process. In the gospel of Luke, look at Jesus at age twelve in the temple, asking questions, and learning. Even at that time He was acting out of the realization of Who His Father was. Jesus' revelation of His identity was not complete by what His parents taught Him. (And neither is ours!)

49

The Scripture reveals He went to the Word of God to continue to understand who He was. He went to the Word of God to affirm and establish His identity. (Not other people!) See a key clue here: This was a habit for Him.

> **"So He came to Nazareth, where He had been brought up. And as His custom was, He went into the synagogue on the Sabbath day, and stood up to read. And He was handed the book of the prophet Isaiah. And when He had opened the book, He found the place where it was written: 'The Spirit of the Lord *is* upon Me, because He has anointed Me to preach the gospel to *the* poor; He has sent Me to heal the brokenhearted, to proclaim liberty to *the* captives and recovery of sight to *the* blind, *to* set at liberty those who are oppressed; to proclaim the acceptable year of the Lord.' Then He closed the book, and gave *it* back to the attendant and sat down. And the eyes of all who were in the synagogue were fixed on Him. And He began to say to them, 'Today this Scripture is fulfilled in your hearing'"** (Luke 4:16-21).

He did not go to the Word to *try* to become the Son of God! He went to the Word to determine and establish Who He already was. Here's our problem: Most of us are trying to become instead of believing who we already are—in Christ. We need to read the Word of God to determine and establish our identity as a child (son or daughter) of God.

I need to have security and peace in being God's daughter. Although I may wear many hats, I can never safely allow them to become my identity or I will always be on a roller coaster of emotions based on my false image of myself.

In His greatest hour of need, just before His crucifixion, when Jesus' identity was most severely tested, every man deserted Him. He faced a horrible death ALONE...a death that came about because of His identity. The Jews even requested that these words be written above His cross, *"He said He was king of the Jews"* trying to insinuate that He was not who He said He was. There on the Cross, His tormentors continued until the bitter end, saying, "If You are who

You say You are, why doesn't God rescue You? Just give us some kind of sign, and we'll be glad to let You be our King." If Jesus had fallen to their temptation to prove identity by works, we'd all be lost! His identity and worth were never determined by the responses of people. He looked totally to God for the acceptance He needed.

I have renewed my thinking to who God made me to be. Layers of who I thought I was, or what I felt others thought about me, could be peeled off. I can just be me, and get to know who that person is as I get to know God in me. Documenting these profound, valuable truths in my heart through biblical meditation has brought about a transformation. I don't want to oversimplify this, but the destiny within has effortlessly emerged out of a settled and established heart. It's an unfolding blueprint day by day!

Chapter 5
Babies

"Oooh, just the very cutest, aren't they?" Yes. Unless, of course, it's a grown man acting like a baby. A baby learns to sit first before they begin to stand and walk. The Christian life also starts with sitting. In all of this, God is positioning us! He…

> "…**Raised *us* up together, and made *us* sit together in the heavenly *places* in Christ Jesus**" (Ephesians 2:6).

Beginnings, birth, babies, maturity and growth are introduced and foretold here.

Personally, I was so hungry to learn in my experience as a new believer. Yet, it was challenging to read the Bible without some clarity, especially with mixed messages coming from most pulpits. Before the Cross of Christ is the Old Covenant, and after His death, burial, and resurrection there is a New Covenant. I needed to grasp that there were two separate covenants and where I fit in. I needed to know about this differentiation before I could make an application to my own life. Otherwise there were too many unanswered questions looming over me. After my initial 'forgiveness of sin' experience, religious tradition left me guilty for not performing up to God's standards.

Finally, I understood this: Paul said…

"For he raised us from the dead along with Christ and seated us with him in the heavenly realms because we are united with Christ Jesus" (Colossians 2:6 NLT).

Jesus fulfilled Old Testament prophecies. He brought the gospel of peace, which is peace between God and man, through His birth, life, death, and resurrection (see Luke 2). Comprehending this distinction between Old and New Covenants has contributed so much to my life as a believer. Learning these new creation realities has positioned me in Christ—sitting far above with a bird's eye view.

As a young woman, filled with the Holy Spirit, this foundational understanding opened up my soul to revelation insights into the Scripture. I began to gain personal directives from reading the Word daily. I enjoyed my time with the Lord and started to journal things He would speak to me. Using my new prayer language deepened my connection with Jesus and His guidance in my life.

A Sign for Generations

We are encouraged to never despise small beginnings (see Zechariah 4:10). Everything has its initial seed form of the growth process. In the unfolding picture of our life of rest, there is the simple understanding in the glimpse of creation. In the beginning, we see…

"Thus the heavens and the earth, and all the host of them, were <u>finished</u>. And on the seventh day God ended His work which He had done, and He rested on the seventh day from all His work which He had done. Then God blessed the seventh day and

sanctified it, because in it He rested from all His work which God had created and made" (Genesis 2:1-4, emphasis mine).

Then, in Exodus...

"**Therefore the children of Israel shall keep the Sabbath, to observe the Sabbath throughout their generations *as* a perpetual covenant. It *is* a sign between Me and the children of Israel forever; for *in* six days the LORD made the heavens and the earth, and on the seventh day He rested and was refreshed**" (Exodus 31:16-17).

God was refreshed? Even before the giving of the Law, God blessed the seventh day. Therein lays this principle of rest introduced! Now, don't misunderstand me. In no way am I suggesting or promoting complete inactivity. God rested not because He was tired, but because He was finished. God sees the end from the beginning (see Isaiah 46:10). He's working a plan!

God works, then He rests. Again, He wasn't tired, but He was finished. It's so simple, yet profound. Think of it: God works and then rests. Yet, He ordained mankind to rest, then work. For us, our work flows out of relationship with Him! God loves our dependency on Him, not our self-sufficiency.

New Life Activity

In this chapter, we're considering babies, the birth and growth of new things, and of rest in its beginnings. Galatians is one of my very favorite Bible books. Paul's teaching addresses both spiritual babies and natural babies, and their parallels (more on this in a moment).

My husband and I became very involved in our local church completely across town, and began to participate in a cell group they promoted nearby. Soon we were hosting a home group meeting as an outreach. Invitations went out to our neighborhood and work associates, and people gathered. This remedied our need for re-socialization—we had been party people! We desired others to know the delivering power of God that we had experienced.

I was privileged to stay at home with our children. Dennis launched a construction company. He bid and sold the jobs, and then did the remodeling work. Many families together in our community of believers were in the same boat. Being at home and raising my babies (Neil and Ali were just four years apart) was one of the most wonderful times of my life. However, I felt like I was enjoying it more than some other friends in my circle.

I loved the priority of our family and social relationships, especially being at home with our kids while they were growing up. We had vehicles paid off, and weren't over our heads in debt or other financial burdens. God was showing Himself so faithful to meet our needs. I stayed active, but tried to make sure the kids got their rest too. Naptime was a good time daily, which can apply to our spiritual life too!

Learning to Walk

I love Bill Murray's goofy movie **What About Bob?** In the silly story, Dr. Marvin advises the obnoxious character "Bob" to take baby steps—setting small reasonable goals—one tiny step at a time to not get overwhelmed. I see that God has tried to give us baby steps all along to comprehend His plan of trusting Him through rest.

Hebrews 4:1-11 talks about a Sabbath rest that is available to, but not necessarily functional in, all New Testament believers. This New Covenant Sabbath rest is simply a relationship with God in which we cease from doing things by our own efforts and let God work through us. The Old Testament Sabbath presents a perfect picture of the New Testament relationship. The Sabbath illustrates a relationship with God that Jesus has now opened up to all who believe. Back then, it was only a picture. Now, that picture is fulfilled in Christ (more on Hebrews 4 later).

I think we need to give a naptime to every burden, worry, anxiety, and care. Put it to bed! As we rest in a trusting way with God and His promises to us, He can show Himself strong on our behalf (see 2 Chronicles 16:9; 2 Corinthians 12:9). How well we learn to walk as a believer depends on how well we sit and rest in the finished work of Christ. Remember, we are seated in heavenly places in Christ!

The apostle Paul expressed these truths of the grace of God like no one else could. These insights have even unveiled to me how God sees discipline for us, His children.

> **"But before faith came, we were kept under guard by the law, kept for the faith which would afterward be revealed. Therefore the law was our tutor *to bring us* to Christ, that we might be justified by faith. But after faith has come, we are no longer under a tutor"** (Galatians 3:23-25).

The Greek word translated **"tutor"** describes a slave in either Greek or Roman households whose job it was to conduct a young child to and from school (to the real teacher), as well as to supervise the life and morals of the child until they reached maturity.

Although the **"tutor"** might instruct, their real job was to supervise by strict enforcement of rules and regulations. So until Christ came the Law was like someone trying to make us behave. The Old Testament Law drove us to holiness to show us the futility of self-salvation. This prepared us for the message of Christ bringing salvation as a gift.

Early childhood development rapidly changes in infants as they grow into toddlerhood. What would be the comparison in spiritual development? How do we define spiritual maturity or immaturity? What would be a true Bible baby? Can you say, "Got milk?"

> **"We have much to say, and hard to explain, since you have become dull of hearing. For though by this time you ought to be teachers, you need *someone* to teach you again the first principles of the oracles of God; and you have come to need milk and not solid food.**

For everyone who partakes *only* of milk *is* unskilled in the word of righteousness, for he is a babe" (Hebrews 5:11-13).

How telling? You need someone to teach you again, which means you didn't get it the first time. If we don't comprehend the free gift of God—that we are made righteous by faith in Jesus, not works—then we are unskilled in the word of righteousness and only drinking milk. Not understanding our righteousness in Christ—by grace through faith—will keep us immature!

If we polled a random group of Christians, their definitions for "spiritual maturity" would be thousands of miles apart. Yet, this key point is crucial to our spiritual foundation (see Hebrews 6:1-3). If we don't get this, everything we build upon it will be crooked. Consider this...

"You're like children still needing milk and not yet ready to digest solid food. For every spiritual infant who lives on milk is not yet pierced by the revelation of righteousness" (Hebrews 5:12-13 TPT).

Have you been pierced yet by the revelation of righteousness? Being permitted to go on to maturity first requires the receiving of certain revelation—righteousness.

"As newborn babes, desire the pure milk of the word that you may grow thereby, if indeed you have tasted that the Lord *is* gracious" (1 Peter 2:2-3).

These scripture references to 'milk' reveal so much about our nourishment as believers. Just as a newborn benefits most by a mama's breast milk, so do we spiritually. There's no need for additives or fillers. When we add our man-made doctrines and preferences to the simple gospel we are risking stunting the growth of the young believer. That gets us stuck. Yet righteousness is a free gift. We need to understand this on a heart level to be able to truly mature in Christ.

Why would we lead anyone to believe anything else, since we have tasted—personally experienced—that the Lord is gracious? Are young believers' spiritual progress being subverted through manipulation and religious bondage? Imagine a caricature of a spiritual baby in the form of an old, white-haired man having to part his beard for a baby's bottle of milk. Well, that happens when people who have been born again a long time ago never get the foundation of their right-standing in Christ as a new believer. How tragic! Spiritual babyhood is a stage to mature out of, not stay in for the rest of your life.

We had to realize this too! We had to pull our thumbs out of our mouths, and put on our big-boy and big-girl pants. Maturity comes through believing the truth that we have been made the righteousness of God in Christ Jesus, and then acting on it. Actively receiving God's love made us secure and whole. Knowing and experiencing the love of Christ brought hope and stability. This is available for you too!

Honestly, more fruit has been developed and abundantly produced in our lives on accident just by having these foundations laid in our hearts. God's approval motivates us. Knowing His acceptance empowers us. This eliminates any insecure need we may have to measure ourselves through comparison to other people.

We are full-grown children of God—sons in Christ. He sees Himself in us. He's not punishing us. We may punish ourselves through dealing with the consequences of our decisions and actions, but our heavenly Father isn't holding anything against us. Thinking God is and does keeps us in an infantile relationship with Him. The Scripture clearly depicts chastening as the process for training a beloved or favored child. Not punishment!

> **"My son, do not despise the chastening of the Lord, nor detest His correction; for whom the Lord loves He corrects, just as a father the son *in whom* he delights"** (Proverbs 3:11).

We are not complacent, staying sensitive to the Holy Spirit as we invest in our hearts. Only those who have known the oppression of the law mentality can fully appreciate the gracious redemption provided by Jesus as a gift. The Old Testament Law gave standards which were enforced by punishments. But for you and me, as New Covenant believers, it's immature to try to relate to God on the basis of punishment and judgment today. Paul shared that...

"Until the time when we were mature enough to respond freely in faith to the living God, we were carefully surrounded and protected by the Mosaic law. The law was like those Greek tutors, with which you are familiar, who escort children to school and protect them from danger or distraction, making sure the children will really get to the place they set out for. But now you have arrived at your destination: By faith in Christ you are in direct relationship with God. Your baptism in Christ was not just washing you up for a fresh start. It also involved dressing you in an adult faith wardrobe—Christ's life, the fulfillment of God's original promise" (Galatians 3:23-27 MSG).

Here we are, back at the righteousness wardrobe! Are you persuaded yet that you have been clothed in Christ? If you could just understand your position of righteousness, you'd be unstoppable! We discovered this truth years ago, and have been living in the reality of it more and more since. What a difference it makes in everything!

"For the grace of God that brings salvation has appeared to all men, teaching us that, denying ungodliness and worldly lusts, we should live soberly, righteously, and godly in the present age" (Titus 2:11-12).

We are no longer slaves to sin! Grace removes our excuses to sin and teaches us to deny—say 'NO' to—sin.

"Now I say *that* the heir, as long as he is a child, does not differ at all from a slave, though he is master of all, but is under guardians and stewards until the time appointed by the father. Even so we, when we were children, were in bondage under the elements of the world. But when the fullness of the time had come, God sent forth His Son, born of a woman, born under the law, to redeem those who were under the law, that we might receive the adoption as sons." (Galatians 4:1-5).

The Law was our tutor for a time, before faith came. Now, time's up!

Sons vs Slaves

Paul gave an illustration to show the state of spiritual immaturity that one experiences by being under the Law. He stated that being under the Law is no better than being a slave, whereas faith in Christ brings us into a position of a full-grown son. It is sad to say, but most Christians have never graduated into the sonship that Paul described here in Galatians. They are still serving God with an Old Testament law mentality which is not pleasing to God and is oppressive to them. Jesus said it was a slave mindset. Sonship is ours. This is who we are. It's been provided for us freely through Christ. But it doesn't happen automatically. We have to renew our minds to take advantage of this privileged relationship (Life for Today Commentary, Andrew Wommack).

We were constantly being told what to do and actually had no freedom to choose. Through Christ, we have been redeemed from the slave relationship to the Law and are now sons with all the rights and privileges, responsibilities and freedoms that go with that.

Understanding righteousness by faith is the measuring stick, the plumb line, the basis for any topic that might be taught or preached. Thus, we lie at the crossroads of fulfilling our true destiny as God intends. We aren't achieving it with self-willed focus. Our response comes from a heart of love and trust in Him for what He's already done. We no longer operate from fear of having to do everything correctly. Right living will emerge effortlessly from a renewed mind and heart by divine enablement.

Maturity as Sons

"And because you are sons, God has sent forth the Spirit of His Son into your hearts, crying out, "Abba, Father!" Therefore you

60

are no longer a slave but a son, and if a son, then an heir of God through Christ" (Galatians 4:6-7).

We are redeemed <u>from</u> the slave relationship BUT are now adopted as sons! He redeemed us TO something! We are redeemed from punishment, wrath and rejection, slavery and bondage to laws, rules, and regulations. But even more, we are brought into a relationship and made an heir of the Master! Receiving blessings for one's own righteousness was the basic premise of the Old Covenant. That's the way unregenerate man related to a Holy God. However, man could never be made righteous by his own works, hence, the need for Jesus to come and give the free gift of righteousness.

As Dr. Jim Richards wrote in his masterful *Foundations of Faith* manual, "Faith-righteousness is the cornerstone or capstone of the gospel. When you build an archway, there is a stone in the center of the archway shaped a certain way. That stone determines if it is all going to hold together. If that capstone or keystone falls out, the whole doorway is going to come down. The foundations of faith provide us with our foundation. There is one thing that holds it together causing it to make sense, and that's faith righteousness. Until a person is established in this they will never find that hub, that matrix, around which everything else fits together."

I've found it, and I pray you find it too!

Chapter 6
Heirs

Heirlooms are family possessions handed down from generation to generation. Being an "heir" means there's an inheritance coming from somewhere. In that respect, I guess I'm an heiress. What a blessing! I was left an inheritance by my dear Mother upon her death. As believers, do we really grasp what's been passed on to us? It's so much more than just finances. God reveals and demonstrates His own generous nature and intention to us through His Son and what He accomplished. Remember, what cost one generation dearly often costs the next generation nothing. Will we properly value what we've been given?

As we receive a heritage, we need to recognize the responsibility bestowed upon us. We must be willing to accept the fact we may spend our lives building something, and then it's the next generation's decision to advance with what we laid down for them.

> **"A good *man* leaves an inheritance to his children's children, but the wealth of the sinner is stored up for the righteous"** (Proverbs 13:22).

God's very nature is generous!

"Ask God for wisdom and he will give it! He won't see your lack of wisdom as an opportunity to scold you over your failures but he will overwhelm your failures with his generous grace" (James 1:5 TPT).

Family Heritage

In our family's journey of coming into destiny, there's been progress in my relationship with the Lord. I want that for you too! So it's with zeal and heartfelt passion that I pray you would grasp the rich deposit of God's Spirit within you, and walk on into the fullness of His purpose and your destiny—through no human striving of your own. It all hinges on the capacity of your heart to believe and receive His willingness to be good to you.

You do cooperate, of course! Picture yourself in a lawyer's office. You're there for the reading of a will. If today was the bequeathal of an estate, you'd have to show up to know what was left for you. Perhaps you're right in the middle of all the pain from your loss, but you have enough of a sense of honor and respect for the deceased to cooperate with the executor—to go find out what rightfully belongs to you. Surely, you recognize there's been a coordination of the lasting legacy available drawn up with you in mind. As it unfolds, it may not be the perfect picture you would want to paint. Perhaps there is some 'coloring outside the lines' in your family tree. Do we value those who have gone before us laying a spiritual heritage? It may or may not have been relatives by blood.

I'm honored in that I did have a wonderful heritage spiritually by a mother who knew God's restoring love in her life. She was in a life-long search for God. Her curious attempts with empty religion and its formalities didn't fill the void. Exploring the occult for supernatural power proved to be a counterfeit that only made things worse, whether through astrology, hypnotism, or cults. She came to the Lord right when we became teenagers. God is so faithful—He finds us!

My Mom prayed to receive forgiveness and came to know Jesus personally through Billy Graham on television. Nearly that same time, my stepfather became radically saved and delivered from alcoholism while in rehab. Allowing God to restore them, and through serving Him with their unique gifts, He made an impact on their lives and through their lives to so many others. My parents hosted a weekly youth meeting in our home, which exposed our entire junior high school to hearing the gospel through the guest evangelists who came.

For nearly a decade, Mom produced a Christian television program with a small team of women. She also had a love for Israel and Jewish people coming to know their Messiah. Mom devoted her energy and talents to build and bless the kingdom of God. As a successful businesswoman, she had a heart for helping others and launching them into their careers with her corporate recruiting firm. To me, her life exemplifies this whole concept of the heritage God has for us if we will believe and let Him move us into action working in and through us.

All of us are most familiar in seeing ourselves and our shortcomings. We often feel inadequate and unqualified. I have good news—He qualified us! We cannot qualify ourselves. Speaking as a witness with firsthand experience, in our helpless state the Lord enriched our lives in every area—family living, parenting, financially, socially, etc. When no one around us believed in us, God did!

Before my mother passed away, even in a weakened state of health, she traveled with me to Chicago meet my first granddaughter—Maliyah—right after her birth. She was her first great granddaughter. Mom was able to hold her in her arms, and we prayed over her together. She was such a welcomed baby girl! Mom passed away just two months later, but not before she attended my son's wedding and celebrated the very-soon-coming second grandchild (of mine) too. She even knew his name would be Joaquin, which means "raised by Yahweh." This was a meaningful time for us.

Not only do we receive heirlooms of jewelry, vases, or furniture, we also pass down spiritual family heirlooms of our values and life of faith in Christ. Mom left a legacy in more ways than one. We are the benefactors of her believing God's promises on our behalf, gratefully aware of how she devoted herself to much prayer for her family in the middle season of her life.

I've spent many hours late at night researching ancestry. It's so intriguing! To consider that we can often do what no other generation has been able to do: Trace our lineage hundreds of years back. Admittedly, this holds no interest for many people. Personally, I like to think of meeting some of these ancestors in heaven. There is a value to the heritage of those who have gone before us—both naturally and spiritually. We have a heritage in the Word of God! You don't have to learn everything by hard knocks.

How then should we live? Choosing personal responsibility is the only pathway to freedom. We must stay dependent upon the Holy Spirit! Look at our inheritance being expressed in a prayer by Paul...

> **"I pray that the light of God will illuminate the eyes of your imagination, flooding you with light, until you experience the full revelation of the hope of his calling—that is, the wealth of God's glorious inheritances that he finds in us, his holy ones!"** (Ephesians 1:18 TPT).

We are His inheritance! God has found treasure in us, even when we aren't aware of it. If we would just get over ourselves, God could really do something through us. He has a personal investment in us fulfilling our purpose and destiny!

Glitch alert:

> **"Yes, and all who desire to live godly in Christ Jesus will suffer persecution"** (2 Timothy 3:12).

That's true, but it doesn't mean that we need to adopt a 'persecution complex' where we live in expectation of it all the time. In the Old Testament, the story of the lives of Isaac and Ishmael in the book of Genesis helps us see the enemy's tactic to try to stop God's people from inheriting effortlessly.

> **"Now you, brothers and sisters, like Isaac, are children of promise.**

At that time the son born according to the flesh persecuted the son born by the power of the Spirit. It is the same now" (Galatians 4:28 NIV).

The child of Law always persecutes the child of grace. It's never the child of grace that persecutes the child of the Law. I once heard Joseph Prince, another fellow minister of God's unconditional love, remark, *"There's almost like a religious hatred for the teaching of grace and it is frightening."* This statement got me thinking and connecting the dots.

There's so much drama and trauma in the recent news…

"Why do the nations rage, and the people plot a vain thing? The kings of the earth set themselves, and the rulers take counsel together, against the Lord and against His Anointed, *saying…*" (Psalm 2:1-2).

While instead, we should move by compassion and be constrained by the love of Christ—not works or Law! God has inheritance for us through Christ—He just wants us to ask for it…

"Ask of Me, and I will give *You* the nations *for* Your inheritance, and the ends of the earth *for* Your possession" (Psalm 2:8).

The devil does not want God's people to inherit effortlessly! Watch closely for the shadow and substance revealed to us through the life story of Abraham's wives—Sarah and Hagar. Here's a question for you…

"Tell me, you who want to be under the law, are you not aware of what the law says? For it is written that Abraham had two sons, one by the slave woman and the other by the free woman. His son by the slave woman was born according to the flesh, but his son by the free woman was born as the result of a divine promise" (Galatians 4:21-23).

These two women represent two covenants, and the two children represent a work of the flesh and a work of the Spirit. The two women are Abraham's wives, Sarah and Hagar. Actually, Sarah was Abraham's wife and Hagar was her

Egyptian handmaiden (slave, see Genesis 16:1). Up to that point Sarah had been barren, so she suggested that Abraham have a sexual relationship with Hagar, and Sarah would raise the child as her own (see Genesis 16:2). This was a common practice of their day. So Abraham did as Sarah wished, and Hagar had a child named Ishmael (Genesis 16:4, 11). God made it clear that this was not the child He had promised to Abraham through whom He would fulfill His promise (see Genesis 17:20-21). About fourteen years after the birth of Ishmael, Abraham and Sarah had a child supernaturally whom they named Isaac (see Genesis 21:1-3).

Ishmael, the son of Hagar, persecuted Isaac, the son of Sarah, to the degree that Sarah begged Abraham to send Hagar and her son Ishmael away (see Genesis 21:9-10). Abraham didn't want to do this, but God spoke to him and told him to do as Sarah had said (see Genesis 21:11-12).

From this story laid out in Genesis, Paul interpreted the significance of these actions in the book of Galatians. Ishmael was a product of self-effort, just as any trust in the Law for the purpose of justification—being made righteous in God's sight—would be. In contrast, Isaac was supernatural. Both Abraham and Sarah were well beyond the age of having children, so Isaac was a miracle. Simply put, salvation by grace is a miracle, not self-effort!

In the same way that Hagar and her son—who was a product of the flesh—were cast out, so those who seek to be justified by the Law are rejected by God. But those who believe the gospel and receive salvation as a gift are like Isaac, who came supernaturally through the promise of God.

So Paul shows us that the truths of the gospel were present in the Old Testament Law, but the legalistic Jews had been blinded to these simple truths. They had misinterpreted the purpose of the Old Testament Law and were therefore wrongfully teaching that conformity to the Law was necessary for salvation. Peter spoke of people who were willfully ignorant of the truth (see 2 Peter 3:5). Paul said in Galatians 3:1 that legalism is crazy. (The Living Commentary, Andrew Wommack)

Who's Your Mama?

Unwrapping this allegory from God's Word will enrich a depth of understanding in your heart that will never be sabotaged by confusion or misunderstanding again...

> **"These things are being taken figuratively: <u>The women represent two covenants</u>. One covenant is from Mount Sinai and bears children who are to be slaves: This is Hagar. <u>Now Hagar stands for Mount Sinai in Arabia and corresponds to the present city of Jerusalem, because she is in slavery with her children. But the Jerusalem that is above is free, and she is our mother</u>"** (Galatians 4:24-26 NIV, emphasis mine).

Compare this with The Message version...

> **"The two births represent two ways of being in relationship with God. One is from Mount Sinai in Arabia. It corresponds with what is now going on in Jerusalem—a slave life, producing slaves as offspring. This is the way of Hagar. In contrast to that, there is an invisible Jerusalem, a free Jerusalem, and she is our mother—this is the way of Sarah"** (Galatians 4:24-26 MSG).

Hagar represents Mount Sinai, where Moses received the Law, and the present (in Paul's time) city of Jerusalem, which was enslaved to Rome as well as to the Law. Hagar's children being slaves corresponds to the Jews' bondage of being under the Law. Jerusalem...

> **"The center of that system of trying to please God by trying to obey the Commandments"** (Galatians 4:25 TLB).

The earthly city of Jerusalem was corrupt. Its inhabitants rejected Jesus by crucifying Him, and they, as a whole, had also rejected the gospel. But the heavenly city of God—of which the earthly Jerusalem was supposed to symbolize—was pure and free. Those who receive salvation by faith in what

Christ did for us, instead of what we do for Him through the Law, are all citizens of this heavenly Jerusalem.

Sing Before You See It

"For it is written: 'Be glad, barren woman, you who never bore a child; shout for joy and cry aloud, you who were never in labor; because more are the children of the desolate woman than of her who has a husband'" (Galatians 4:27 NIV).

This verse is a quotation Isaiah 54:1 from the Septuagint, which is the Greek translation of the Old Testament. The **"barren"** in this verse refers to Sarah. The Lord told her to break forth into singing and rejoicing before she became pregnant. The barren Sarah rejoiced at the promise of God through faith (see Hebrews 11:11) and through the promised seed (Christ, see Galatians 3:16) she had infinitely more children than her slave Hagar (all believers are Abraham's seed). Just as Isaac was conceived supernaturally, so the Galatians became God's children, not through their own efforts, but totally through a supernatural work of God.

"Now you, brothers and sisters, like Isaac, are children of promise. At that time the son born according to the flesh persecuted the son born by the power of the Spirit. It is the same now. But what does Scripture say? "Get rid of the slave woman and her son, for the slave woman's son will never share in the inheritance with the free woman's son." Therefore, brothers and sisters, we are not children of the slave woman, but of the free woman" (Galatians 4:28 NIV).

In the same way that Ishmael persecuted Isaac, the child of promise (see Genesis 21:9), so it is now. Those who rely on the flesh (the Law) persecute those born of the Spirit (who have been saved by grace). There have always been, and until Jesus returns, will always be only two kinds of religion—those of faith (grace) and those of works (Law). Those of Law will always continue to persecute those of grace, just like Cain did toward Abel (see Genesis 4:3-8).

Paul took the Galatians back to the Scriptures, speaking from Genesis 21:9-14. Just as Hagar and Ishmael will not have any part in the inheritance of Isaac, so those of the covenant of Law with its legalism will not inherit the promise of justification which comes by faith. The apostle was saying that we do not obtain right standing with God through the Law (**"the slave woman,"** Hagar), but through faith (**"the free woman,"** Sarah).

Children of Great Promise

Only after I felt loved could I make others feel loved. From that feeling of loving myself and being loved by God, people around me began to be established in worth. You are worth the amount of love God bestows upon you. However, you must believe and feel that love for it to affect your life. Like Dave Duell would always say, *"The person who will affect your life the most isn't the person you believe in; it's the person who believes in you!"* God believes in you! He is no respecter of persons. The revelation shared in these stories propels us into a greater trusting of our good, good Father. Settle this in your heart. Because of being in Christ, the seed of Abraham, we are children of promise and Jerusalem from above (God's grace, divine ability) is our Mother.

> **"So in Christ Jesus you are all children of God through faith, for all of you who were baptized into Christ have clothed yourselves with Christ. There is neither Jew nor Gentile, neither slave <u>nor free, nor is there male and female,</u> for <u>you are all one in Christ Jesus</u>"** (Galatians 3:26, emphasis mine).

Distinctions created by religious Law that separated Jew and Gentile, male and female, and so on, no longer exist in Christ Jesus. That is profound! Through union with the Lord we have all been made one. We are one new man, the body of Christ, joined together by faith in Jesus (see Ephesians 1:22-23).

70

Jesus' purpose in coming into the world was twofold. First, He came to redeem those who were under the Law. Think of how He did that by perfectly keeping the Law, fulfilling it, and paying its curse. So Christ delivered us from the entire system of the Law. The Greek word for "redeem" means to buy out of the slave market. This system of Law was then superseded by grace, with an emphasis on living by faith. You and I were slaves set free to be sons! So secondly, Christ gave us the status of sonship with all its privileges. In the Greek, the expression means adult sons. Under grace, we're treated as adults, not babies!

Sonship

"If you belong to Christ, then you are Abraham's seed, and heirs according to the promise" (Galatians 4:29).

We discover that God's promises were made to Abraham and his seed— Christ. Christ participated in the covenant agreement on our behalf. Jesus had no need of being justified through faith. Therefore, as our representative, the promise was made to Him, and since we are "in Him" we receive the benefits. We're also guaranteed that this covenant will not be voided by our performance because the promise was made to Christ, not to us. We are beneficiaries of His goodness, not ours. And this sonship includes both male and female.

"What I am saying is that as long as an heir is underage, he is no different from a slave, although he owns the whole estate" (Galatians 4:1 NIV).

Think of it—as long as the heir is a child, he does not benefit. We must grow up! But how?

This truth has profoundly impacted me and how I define maturity in spiritual growth. Paul gave a human illustration to show the state of spiritual immaturity that one experiences by being under the Law. I know that righteousness is mine as a free gift. He stated that being under the Law is no better than being a slave,

71

whereas faith in Christ brings us into a position of a full-grown son (see Galatians 3:26). Will you believe it?

We are redeemed from the slave relationship but, even more impacting, now that we are adopted as sons, He redeemed us TO something! Think of it this way, in two steps: We are redeemed from punishment, wrath and rejection, slavery and bondage to laws, rules, and regulations; as we are brought into a relationship and made an heir of the Master! We have to renew our minds to take advantage of this blessed relationship. We must deal with our own mentality or belief system. Paul's life message and prayer for us was passing on inheritance…

> **"And so now, I entrust you into God's hands and the message of his grace, which is all that you need to become strong. All of God's blessings are imparted through the message of his grace, which he provides as the spiritual <u>inheritance</u> given to all of his holy ones"** (Acts 20:32 TPT, emphasis mine).

This has become my life message too—God's grace makes us able!

Everything Is Already Yours!

In the prodigal son story, the father told the older brother, in essence, "Son, you are always with me, and I am always with you. All I have is yours!" (see Luke 15:31) As a generation of people start to recognize the inheritance they have, they will begin to rise. And in that rising their level of interaction with the generation who gave them the inheritance will increase. It's really important to understand that inheritance is never about what we have done. It's all about who we are and what we believe!

Instead of being divided into people camps, we need to recognize our true focus is on Jesus the center of it all. Of course, we have our preferences of who is influencing us, but we need to esteem the gifts in all and one another. Paul put it all in perspective and put down man's wisdom to stop division. Ministry gifts coming through individuals are to serve people, not to become a source of strife and petty favoritism among who we're going to follow. Be humble enough to receive from everyone!

> "**Therefore let no one boast in men. For <u>all things are yours</u>: whether Paul or Apollos or Cephas, or the world or life or death, or things present or things to come—<u>all are yours</u>**" (1 Corinthians 3:21-22, emphasis mine).

We are His inheritance. This is our inheritance. Why not pray right now:

Lord, please open my understanding to believe what You are saying to me and receive what you have already done for me. Amen!

Chapter 7
Oasis

Within this rich experience of knowing God is an encounter with all that is an oasis. What's an oasis? It's something serving as a refuge, relief, or pleasant change from what is usual, annoying, or difficult. That sure describes our life without the Holy Spirit—usual, annoying, and difficult. But once we receive His relief and refuge—what a pleasant change!

He is a Fountain, a Well, and a Wellspring. The Lord intends for us all to enter into a life that flows. Our fountains from the Spirit refresh and remind us of the truth on a daily basis.

> **"On the last day, that great *day* of the feast, Jesus stood and cried out, saying, "If anyone thirsts, let him come to Me and drink. He who believes in Me, as the Scripture has said, out of his heart will flow rivers of living water." But this He spoke concerning the Spirit, whom those believing in Him would receive; for the Holy Spirit was not yet *given,* because Jesus was not yet glorified"** (John 7:37-38).

This wonderful ministry takes all the knowledge head-stuffing out of our development process. We can now have a fluid relationship with the Person of the Holy Spirit, Who will bring us refreshing and rest. He convinces us of our right standing in Christ. Now, we know we are forgiven. Yet, self-limiting obstacles try to block our way.

Self-Doubt

We devoted fifteen years of offering our *Life Bible College* training through the ministry of our local church. Through it, we encountered all the hindrances that arise as people sometimes resist seeing themselves how God sees them. Just like the story of Gideon in the Old Testament (who was a military leader, judge, and prophet but), he had a lot of self-doubt when first called by God. Gideon achieved one of the greatest military victories of all time with only 300 men, yet he started out with no confidence in himself.

Are you feeling overlooked? Feeling like you're left out? How are you seeing yourself? If you could take your eyes off of yourself you would be more empowered to move out into what you were created for! Think of his situation: An angel came and sat under a tree while Gideon threshed wheat and complained in a winepress ("whine-press").

"The Angel of the LORD appeared to him, and said to him, 'The LORD *is* with you, you mighty man of valor!'" (Judges 6:12).

His response was much like how ours would be...

"Gideon said to Him, 'O my lord, if the LORD is with us, why then has all this happened to us? And where *are* all His miracles which our fathers told us about, saying, 'Did not the LORD bring us up from Egypt?' But now the LORD has forsaken us and delivered us into the hands of the Midianites.' Then the LORD turned to him and said, 'Go in this might of yours, and you shall save Israel from the hand of the Midianites. Have I not sent you?' So he said to

75

Him, 'O my **LORD,** how can I save Israel? Indeed my clan *is* the weakest in Manasseh, and I *am* the least in my father's house.' And the **LORD** said to him, 'Surely I will be with you, and you shall defeat the Midianites as one man'" (Judges 6:13-16).

It's amazing to read how patient God is with us after all of the doubt and fear expressed. We often have such struggle. He just gets us back on target, emphasizing what He's put in us! "Go in this might of yours, I will be with you and you will win!" God saw Gideon as a mighty man of valor, but it took Gideon time to recognize this for himself.

Misplaced Blame

Too often we clearly blame God for all of our negative life issues. We may not call it that, but we express ourselves the very same way Gideon just did. "If that is God's plan, why did this happen?" 'Why' questions always get us and keep us in a 'stuck' state.

Job blamed God...

"Then the LORD answered Job out of the whirlwind, and said: 'Now prepare yourself like a man; I will question you, and you shall answer Me: Would you indeed annul My judgment? Would you condemn Me that you may be justified?'" (Job 40:6-8).

We must be settled in knowing and experiencing that God is good and trustworthy, and is not our problem. He's the One there to always help us out of every dilemma. God knows who we are and what our capabilities are because He created us.

Finding Your Niche

God has called us into the fellowship of His Son (see 1 Corinthians 1:9). That relationship should have the utmost priority. God gave us a heart-to-heart connection with Him. Prayer is the vehicle, but is designed to be answered through communing honestly heart to heart. Paul spoke from the Spirit His divine guidance to us…

> **"We appeal to you, dear brothers and sisters, to instruct those who are not in their place of battle. *Be skilled at* gently encouraging those who feel themselves inadequate. *Be faithful* to stand your ground. Help the weak to stand again. Be *quick to* demonstrate patience with everyone"** (1 Thessalonians 5:14 TPT).

God may call us to things that haven't even entered our hearts or minds yet. We may think we have well-laid plans but God knows the end from the beginning. Are we open to His directives? Remember, performance-based acceptance from God or others is a diabolical game with no winners and plenty of losers. Those who fail to perform are made to feel like nobodies while those who get the gold stars can end up further from grace than when they started. Most everyone around them is privy to it—even if they aren't. Yet, we don't want to enable codependent issues in our life by our 'needing to be needed,' whether within ourselves or others. That can happen by doing for others what they can (and should) do for themselves. Thus exists the typical situation in most churches.

The sooner we come to know we need a Savior, and that we should remain completely dependent upon Him for everything, the sooner we experience supernatural enablement. Too often we get into toxic unhealthy relationships by expecting something from close friends or family that we have no business expecting. His strength is made perfect in our weakness (see 2 Corinthians 12:9). Our walk of faith is not a competition or a comparison game (see 2 Corinthians 10:12).

I so clearly remember the realization of God's calling to preach and teach the gospel of grace when I knew it wasn't about us, but all about Him. We are not at the center—He is! Life's winners can be its biggest losers if they become addicted to the feeling of being special that comes from accomplishment. Let's make our boast in the Lord! He will bring it to pass if we'll yield.

Gospel Hope Produces Holiness

Paul taught that we are created in righteousness and true holiness...
> **"The new man which was created according to God, in true righteousness and holiness"** (Ephesians 4:24).

It's not something we achieve, but something we're born again into. Regarding holiness, I like the definition of being set apart to God. The actual Greek word translated holiness here means 'a piety toward God.' The Vine's Expository Dictionary defines it as, "the quality of holiness which is manifested in those who have regard equally to grace and truth." In context, Paul was recommending a proper attitude to adopt...
> **"And be renewed in the spirit** [mental disposition (Strong's); attitude (see AMP)] **of your mind, and that you put on the new man which was created according to God, in true righteousness and holiness"** (Ephesians 4:23-24; brackets mine).

We allow the truth of our new nature to change our attitudes and feelings. Understanding the righteous and holy reality of our born-again spirit should adjust our outlook and sentiments. Our perspectives have to change to align with who we are now in Christ.

Holiness is an awesome word, but so often misunderstood. The believer's righteousness and holiness is not something we grow into. We were created that way when we were born again. This righteousness and holiness is in our new spirit which we received from God. Since Paul said "true holiness," this implies there must also be a "false holiness," which would be assumed from the good we do (see Living Commentary, Andrew Wommack).

Paul Ellis states in his writing, "To be holy is to partake of His wholeness; it is to stop acting broken because in Him we are not broken. Allow Him to express

His whole and beautiful life through us. The challenge is that being holy is a new experience for us. As sinners, our lifestyle was characterized by brokenness and hurt. Holy living was alien to us. Now that we are in Him, we have to learn to walk in our new and God-given identity."

Approved & Accepted

Most of my adult life, even as a believer, I thought as though God just tolerated me. I felt He was disappointed with my attitude and behavior. I operated with a constant sense that I really did not measure up. I was trying very hard though and was eager to please God after being so extremely rebellious for a long time in my teens. That was condemnation and shame. Now I know that if I felt that as a dedicated, church-going Christian, there must be tons more people doing the same thing. Something is wrong with this picture! What a waste of valuable time and energy…

"See what great love the Father has lavished on us, that we should be called children of God! And that is what we are! The reason the world does not know us is that it did not know him. Dear friends, now we are children of God, and what we will be has not yet been made known. But we know that when Christ appears, we shall be like him, for we shall see him as he is. All who have this hope in him purify themselves, just as he is pure" (1 John 3:1-3 NIV).

Here is my point: This is our oasis of forgiveness, confidence, identity, acceptance, His approval, holiness, and the ministry of the Holy Spirit. It results in an overflowing harvest! I know this by revelation and personal encounter with the love of God. It's been completely substantiated by God's Word, which gives me confidence and stability. I cannot help but dedicate myself to clearing up this misunderstanding!

You must see yourself as authorized and approved by God. With Holy Spirit's help, I've peeled off the layers of doubt and fear. This experience of the baptism in the Holy Spirit has been one of the most impacting in my entire life- combined with realizing the love and value God has for me has enhanced a flourishing and blossoming into purpose. God smiles on our rite of passage into adulthood from His Son who accomplished everything for us. Like everything with grace, His acceptance and approval is a free gift that comes to us through Christ alone.

"To the praise of the glory of His grace, by which He made us accepted in the Beloved" (Ephesians 1:6). Do you feel His acceptance?

That's very good news for those who want no part in the 'earning acceptance' game. Look back at the first part of that verse. Does the Word say, "To the praise of the glory of your service"? No, it doesn't. His acceptance of you is "**to the praise of the glory of *His grace*.**" Isn't that wonderful?

But wait, it gets better. Look at the middle part of that verse. "**He *made* us** [past tense] **accepted.**" His acceptance is not something you ever need to strive for; you already have it. What a relief! What freedom! This is fundamental, and served as another key in bringing me such release from the performance trap. Every time I think of this I'm free to be myself. And it enables me to treat everyone around me the same way.

But hold on, there's more. Look at the final part of the verse: "**in the Beloved.**" This is referring to Jesus. God's acceptance comes to you on account of His Son. So if you want to know just how acceptable you are to God, you only have to look at the One called, "**Beloved.**" You were forgiven in accordance with the riches of God's grace.

"In Him we have redemption through His blood, the forgiveness of sins, according to the riches of His grace" (Ephesians 1:7).

What is the limiting measure of God's forgiveness? Is it our achievements, or the state of our confession? No! We are forgiven according to the riches of God's grace. God is not stingy with grace. The Scriptures teach He even gives MORE grace!

"But He gives more grace. Therefore He says: 'God resists the proud, but gives grace to the humble'" (James 4:6).

Notice that Jesus received His Father's verbal endorsement and approval openly <u>before</u> He ever performed a miracle when He was baptized in the river. Now we are in Christ. We are approved when we believe.

"When He had been baptized, Jesus came up immediately from the water; and behold, the heavens were opened to Him, and He saw the Spirit of God descending like a dove and alighting upon Him. And suddenly a voice *came* **from heaven, saying, 'This is My beloved Son, in whom I am well pleased'"** (Matthew 3:16-17).

Let this Bible story aid you in uprooting any wrong beliefs. Re-document the truth in your heart from these verses. As Peter preached in the book of Acts, he emphasized how Jesus was approved with signs following His ministry…

"Men of Israel, hear these words: Jesus of Nazareth, a Man attested by God to you by miracles, wonders, and signs which God did through Him in your midst, as you yourselves also know" (Acts 2:22).

Peter was saying that God bore witness to the authenticity of who Jesus was by the miracles which He performed through Him. If Jesus needed the miraculous power of God to bear witness to His words, then how much more do we? The Greek word translated "attested" in this verse means 'to demonstrate, accredit, approve, set forth, show.' Through believing, we can expect to live a life with manifestations of miraculous power. We are in Christ and approved!

We have gone from infancy to maturity by believing we are righteous. This gives us a life launching pad. What began to happen in my own life was my own identity in Christ and divine purpose began to emerge like hidden treasure pulled up from a sunken ship. These are the very stepping stones I walked upon to come out of fear, insecurity, and low self-worth. My mind has been renewed and my heart experiences joy every time I think of this oasis of forgiveness, confidence, identity, acceptance, God's approval and holiness in me in Christ.

Storytellers

We can LOSE ourselves in a story. Our hearts will grasp a truth that causes a miraculous change. This is exactly what Jesus did with parables. He used the language of the day. He told stories about things people understood, such as farming, shepherding, vineyards, and weather. The Lord used allegory to get people to subconsciously draw parallels between divine principles and natural occurrences. Having removed them from the realm of the mystical and the intellectual, they were able to enter the realm of believing, and thereby experience the miraculous. When those people experienced the miraculous, they could tell what happened, but not explain <u>how or why</u>. Like anyone in a desperate situation, when we experience the miracle we need, the how and why is of little concern. The experience is everything!

"Believing is not an intellectual happening. It is something that occurs at the heart level. It is something that happens so deeply that it affects the way we think and feel. It alters the way we see ourselves. It happens instantaneously and without effort. It can be grasped but not learned. It can be experienced but not earned!" A quote from Dr. Jim Richards' teaching.

What Is Born of God?

"Dear friends, let us love one another, for love comes from God. Everyone who loves has been born of God and knows God. Whoever does not love does not know God, because God is love" (1 John 4:7-8 NIV).

Now, we are Daddy's little girl (or boy) all grown up!

Sowing the Seed

I've been transformed through meditating on and renewing my mind to the truth of God's Word. Too much attention on visible growth in a person will cause us to become impatient and not take the time to become firmly established

82

in the truths of God's Word. This will always result in fruitlessness. A seed planted in shallow earth will germinate and grow faster than a seed planted in deep soil. The seed in deep soil will put all of its energy toward the roots first while the seed in shallow soil has no choice but to put its effort into the growth of the plant above the ground. This works exactly the same in the life of a person being a disciple in the kingdom of God. The plant in shallow soil will look like it is far ahead of the other seed for a while but that will not last. It soon withers and dies, while the seed with roots grows to maturity and brings forth fruit.

Some Christians get very excited over the promises of God's Word but make the mistake of not getting firmly established in those truths before they 'jump out on a limb' with them. This kind of person withers away when the heat is on. We can't live off of someone else's revelation of or commitment to the Word. We must have root in ourselves! No one can do it for us. Then act on what you believe.

> **"And some are like the seed that lands in the gravel. When they first hear the Word, they respond with great enthusiasm. But there is such shallow soil of character that when the emotions wear off and some difficulty arrives, there is nothing to show for it"** (Mark 4:16-17 MSG).

The Growing Seed

Remember, Jesus was never without a story! He used them to enlighten the clueless…

> **"'Are you listening to this? Really listening? Listen carefully to what I am saying—and be wary of the shrewd advice that tells you how to get ahead in the world on your own. Giving, not getting, is the way. Generosity begets generosity. Stinginess impoverishes.' Then Jesus said, 'God's kingdom is like seed thrown on a field by a man <u>who then goes to bed and forgets about it</u>. The seed sprouts**

and grows—he <u>has no idea how it happens</u>. **The earth does it all without his help: first a green stem of grass, then a bud, then the ripened grain. When the grain is fully formed, he reaps—harvest time! How can we picture God's kingdom? What kind of story can we use? It's like a pine nut. When it lands on the ground it is quite small as seeds go, yet once it is planted it grows into a huge pine tree with thick branches. Eagles nest in it"** (Mark 4:23-32 MSG, emphasis mine).

You don't have to wonder 'why' anymore! This so beautifully depicts the process of how seed sowing and growing has been going on when you were completely unaware of it. It paints a kingdom picture so accurate that we must grasp it to grow emotionally and spiritually. A seed is a baby in its own way. You may not know how it's happened but, by your right believing and receiving, the seed has come into full growth with the freedom for you to be you.

This Is a Rest

An oasis is a wellspring or a fountain. It can also mean a small fertile or green area in a desert region, usually having a spring or a well. Thank God for the Holy Spirit living within us! In the Old Testament, the prophet gave us a glimpse of the Spirit's ministry to bring us rest. This included the language of the Spirit, also known as our prayer language...

"To whom He said, 'This *is* the rest *with which* You may cause the weary to rest,' and, 'this *is* the refreshing"; yet they would not hear" (Isaiah 28:12).

Notice how he even prophesied that there would be resistance to it. I pray none of us would resist Him or His refreshing. From His oasis of love we experience forgiveness, confidence, identity, acceptance, approval and holiness.

"Jesus stood and cried out, saying, 'If anyone thirsts, let him come to Me and drink. He who believes in Me, as the Scripture has said, out of his heart will flow rivers of living water'" (John 7:37-38).

Rivers of living water flowing! One of the highlights of life on this planet is the great privilege of allowing the mighty Holy Spirit to pray through us and allow the rivers of living water to flow out of us. This is a rest!

Chapter 8
Lands

"May the LORD give you increase more and more, You and your children. *May* you *be* blessed by the LORD, Who made heaven and earth. The heaven, *even* the heavens, *are* the LORD's; But the earth He has given to the children of men" (Psalm 115:14-16).

After a year of apartment dwelling as newlyweds, we stretched out to find a property to purchase with an old house on it. One of the things I asked the Lord for in my simple prayer request was a large lot of trees. God did it! It was our dream place to live—land for us!

God gave authority on planet earth to man. It has and is becoming what humanity chooses. In an excerpt from Dr. Jim Richards' new book *Heaven on Earth*, he shares about, "when mankind trusted and yielded to God they lived in His perfect will: no sin, sickness or lack of any kind—heaven on earth. Contrary to what religion teaches the curse that came upon the earth was not God's punishment for sin; it was the consequence of man's choices. As man dominated it, he evolved into what he desired... A world ruled by men without God's Commandments or wisdom, hence the Scripture that says **'cursed is the ground because of you.'** It does not say God cursed the earth.

The King James Version clearly states that the earth was cursed for '**your sakes.**' The Hebrew root word for '**your sakes**' points to the changes that occurred in the hearts of Adam and Eve, specifically a change in their perception. It was they who changed their view, most likely referring to their view of God. They no longer believed He was good or worthy of trust." These truths lay important groundwork for understanding so much clearer as we journey to live out our destiny blueprint.

We had our first little cottage home in the midst of trees. We wanted to serve God with our lives and were trusting Him to direct our steps, which He was certainly doing. We renovated that one-hundred-year-old house, had two children there, and hosted a weekly home group from our church. The first five years of living there, we led a Bible study. A ragtag group of us met faithfully together always inviting others. We introduced people to Jesus, prayed with folks, helped divorcees and elderly people, told Bible stories, and hosted crafts and games for children. We served food to friends—and friends of friends—that came our way. It was such a time of growth in our faith!

An indicator of our spiritual maturity and capacity for growth is measured by the degree we can get along and love one another. Don't kid yourself or think too highly of your spirituality if you can't work it out with others, especially those at home. (I'm not referring to or including abusive relationships that people are trapped in.) Knowing we are loved by God is the first step to truly being able to love others.

God Says 'GO'

Stepping out in faith to follow God's Great Commission, we began to 'GO.' God told Abraham to go, saying, "**I *am* the Lord, who brought you out of Ur of the Chaldeans, to give you this land to inherit it**" (Genesis 15:7). So He told us, and we participated in teams annually that would street witness in New Orleans at the Mardi Gras. It turned out to be the best ministry and people training we could ever have received. We learned so much about people through those days and times. We met folks from every walk of life, sharing the gospel one on one countless times, and often in a unique way with each individual personality. Holy Spirit would lead us to tell a story of good news one way to one person and then a completely different way with another. We discovered how God is so very personal, knowing each one of our differences and frailties, and able to reach people right where they're at.

Rest & Refresh

"Therefore the children of Israel shall keep the Sabbath, to observe the Sabbath throughout their generations as a perpetual covenant. It is a sign between Me and the children of Israel forever; for in six days the Lord made the heavens and the earth, and on the seventh day He rested and was refreshed' " (Exodus 31:16-17).

It was God's idea to have physical rest in our week. In fact, we may not think we can afford a vacation, but the truth is as we prioritize what the Lord prioritizes we'll realize we can't afford not to take a vacation from time to time. New places and spaces connect us with new faces. God chose a day of rest. In the cycle of creation, we have an example of one day out of seven for rest. We'd be wise to heed! If our bodies don't rest, it takes its toll on us. It's all so symbolic of the priority God places on relationship and our trust in Jesus. Is He our real Source? Let's think about this. The real me is from the breath of God. I am eternal. Our human spirit doesn't ever cease to exist. But our physical bodies are made from the dust of the ground, which even after the Law God advised to rest the soil (land) every seventh year.

"Then I will command My blessing on you in the sixth year, and it will bring forth produce enough for three years. And you shall

sow in the eighth year, and eat old produce until the ninth year; until its produce comes in, you shall eat *of* the old *harvest*" (Leviticus 25:21-22).

He said that if you honor God, He will supply and bless (1 out of 7 years rest). On the 6th year God commands a blessing and says, "You'll produce a 3 year harvest." Did you know that even today some Israeli farmers rest their ground, yet they remain the largest fruit and flower producers for Europe?

Possessing the Land

God directed the children of Israel to 'possess the land.' That mandate challenges us to trust Him to conquer new territories and advance His kingdom. We are to be on the offensive, constantly taking new ground! Too many believers are passive and defensive, hiding behind the walls of a supposed 'prayer closet.' That's not the posture for God's people. Prayer—yes, of course. But hiding— no. We are to pray and go! The promised land was a land of rest where God promised His people **"large and beautiful cities which you did not build, houses full of all good things, which you did not fill, hewn-out wells which you did not dig, vineyards and olive trees which you did not plant"** (Deuteronomy 6:10-11). However, God's people wandered in the wilderness for 40 years because they refused to believe that He had given them a land where everything had been prepared. The work was finished, but they could not believe that God had given them a land full of riches to enjoy, just flowing with His goodness.

Today there are believers who still can't believe that the work of Jesus is truly complete and finished. They are trying to complete a completed work, finish a finished work, and defeat a defeated devil. There are believers today who are always working and trying to produce their healing, prosperity, success, and victory.

God wants us to stop trying and start trusting in His love for us. He wants us to stop working and struggling, and start resting and believing in His grace toward us. He has finished the work. Our part is to believe and receive. Do you really want another lap around the mountain?

Have you ever been in a life-threatening situation where someone was drowning? When someone desperately flails their arms trying to gasp for air, in their strength they can pull someone else down with them. But when one is tired and weak—when they give up—then they can be rescued. It's much the same with God; when we stop all of our fearful attempts to save ourselves and let go, and rest, He can save us.

Community Makes Creativity Thrive

Our church family collaborating together made not only creativity thrive, but the spiritual impetus of planting a church in our community made new life come alive in a great multiplication of ministry. The church property we purchased blessed many families and has had an ongoing supernatural supply for over twenty years. Our town—Kansas City—is often called the City of Fountains. Fountains represent flourishing, an oasis of refreshing. We—the body of Christ, His Church—are to be that to the world. God uses the promise of lands to be a safe haven for gatherings of His people.

As we began in the 1990s, we met weekly for a Celebration Service with energetic, turned on Jesus-people, who were very excited about what God was doing in our midst. We were preaching the bold good news gospel with signs following the ministry of the Word (and we still are too!). We were just growing in the knowledge of God's unconditional love and grace. As we grasped this simple distinction in the message, sharing it brought transformation as people heard about God loving them first. They began to realize He wasn't mad at them. So many of us take for granted what we have in Jesus, but when we can genuinely celebrate our righteousness in Christ being a free gift, it has a positive domino effect in our lives. So we gained momentum in the Spirit. Our church thrived for the first six years in rented facilities until we found just the right place to purchase. We cast out the vision of a building that would be used to train up and send out people to both our city and the world.

We taught on the radio for eight years while renting meeting spaces and saving money for the time when we would be able to buy a building. God led us to a space on a main drag in our city where there was much traffic. Supernatural provision came together as we began with $40,000 initially saved of the $150,000 needed—just for the down payment for a bank loan. Thank God for a faithful church family rallying together! In less than a month, we had the supernatural finances to put down from a group at the time of less than 150 people. The final day of closing the loan we had the last $10,000. Our trust in God to get into that building continued as we exercised the faith and patience in Him to maintain what He had given us. The Lord has faithfully provided through all the years. It wasn't always easy, but God is a Father, Friend, Shepherd, Deliverer, and Counselor!

We remodeled one room at a time, adding a very trendy little coffee shop that was open for 6 days a week for an entire decade. We served the community, our very dedicated band of believers all cooperating and doing their part in this effective outreach vision. We served breakfast, specialty coffee drinks, and lunch Paninis. We hosted Life Bible Training School for fifteen years. We've gotten a lot of mileage out of our facility, and hundreds and hundreds of people have come in and gone out. God showed Himself strong through an amazing church family that has literally made a world impact through missions, conferences, Bible training, and community outreaches. The body of Christ really needs interdependence upon one another, as well as revelation into kingdom operations—His way of doing things. We have shared that together in a bond of love that has spilled out to touch families all over!

As I write these words today, we are in the unfolding process of selling our facility as we step out in faith into the next phase of ministry with more exploits ahead. Let's consider the ultimate land owner and His intentions to get all of us out into the vineyard where **"whatever is right you will receive"** (Matthew 20:7).

Laborers in the Vineyard

As a land owner, our God is generous. From studying and meditating on the passage of Scripture containing the parable of the laborers in the vineyard, I've learned many meaningful truths that have served me well in life. For instance, I know to stay in my own lane and mind my own business. I've learned to be happy for others and truly deal with my own sense of unfairness, which wasn't based on God's ideas. As we look at this passage, a main point I hope you will take away is how to really experience the goodness of God for yourself, and to see your need for the family of God.

When Jesus taught by parables, He had key truths that He wanted us to grasp. He appealed to our sense of perception, probing to see if we have a heart to understand. This parable of the laborers in the vineyard has always been one of my personal favorites to gain wisdom in how to live relationally and cultivate a heart of generosity without unjust expectations. It's filled with prophetic insight from our Lord, and came as a response to a question from Peter about the sacrifices we think we make for the kingdom of God. Let's follow closely and see where God has positioned us at this time in history!

Are you feeling left out? Do you feel as though you are the least, the last, or the lost? Peter asked Jesus similar questions as to 'how' the kingdom of God worked when the servants (the workers) of the kingdom gave up what they thought was 'so much' for following Jesus...

"Then Peter answered and said to Him, 'See, we have left all and followed You. Therefore what shall we have?'" (Matthew 19:27).

It's almost as though he's asking, "In light of leaving all to follow You, what's in this for us? What gain should we expect for our sacrifice?" Jesus responds by

92

sharing with them this parable. (Keep in mind that Matthew's gospel was written to portray Jesus as the Messiah. He wrote it to Jews who were in great expectation of the kingdom promised in the Old Testament to appear. The Jews were "first" and the Gentiles were "last." The conclusion of this passage is "**So the last will be first, and the first last. For many are called, but few chosen**" (Matthew 20:16). I believe the "**chosen**" ones here are those with the capacity to believe in and receive the generosity of the Master!

I've always known this story as one revealing God's grace and generosity, but I'm seeing more now the scope of a timeline being laid out too. In this parable, there seems to be this 'unfairness' that we can all relate to. Yet, if we have the eyes to see, there's also this refreshing understanding of the goodness of God's heart.

Hundredfold?

> "**Then Peter answered and said to Him, 'See, we have left all and followed You. Therefore what shall we have?' So Jesus said to them, 'Assuredly I say to you, that in the regeneration, when the Son of Man sits on the throne of His glory, you who have followed Me will also sit on twelve thrones, judging the twelve tribes of Israel. And everyone who has left houses or brothers or sisters or father or mother or wife or children or lands, for My name's sake, shall receive a hundredfold, and inherit eternal life. But many *who are* first will be last, and the last first'**" (Matthew 19:27-30, emphasis mine).

As you see the same questions repeated in the parallel passage from Mark below, don't get hung up on the terminology 'one hundredfold' return. Instead, focus on when Jesus said they would receive it. God is preparing us to receive His oceans of grace. Can you expand the capacity of your heart to receive His goodness today?

Now in This Time

"Then Peter began to say to Him, 'See, we have left all and followed You.' So Jesus answered and said, 'Assuredly, I say to you, there is no one who has left house or brothers or sisters or father or mother or wife or children or lands, for My sake and the gospel's, <u>who shall not receive a hundredfold now in this time—</u> houses and brothers and sisters and mothers and children and lands, with persecutions—and in the age to come, eternal life. But many *who are* first will be last, and the last first'" (Mark 10:28-31, emphasis mine).

Remember, Jesus was responding to Peter's question. After His initial answer, the Lord continued with the parable...

"'For the kingdom of heaven is like a landowner [Jesus] who went out <u>early</u> in the morning [before 9am] to hire laborers for his vineyard. Now when he had <u>agreed</u> with the laborers for a denarius a day, he sent them into his vineyard [This could be a time line and reference symbolic to the exactingness of the Law]. And he went out about the <u>third hour</u> [9am] and saw others standing idle in the marketplace, and said to them, 'You also go into the vineyard, and <u>whatever is right I will give you</u>.' So they went [Notice, there was no verbal agreement from proposed workers here at 9am]. Again he went out about the sixth [noon] and the ninth hour [3pm], and <u>did likewise</u> [same with these groups]. And about the eleventh hour [5pm] he went out and found others standing idle, and said to them, 'Why have you been standing here idle all day?' They said to him, 'Because no one hired us.' He said to them, 'You also go into the vineyard, and <u>whatever is right you will receive</u>.' [In the Jewish calendars an evening and morning is one day] So when <u>evening</u> had come, the owner of the vineyard said to his steward, 'Call the

94

laborers and give them *their* wages, <u>beginning with the last to the first</u>.' And when those came who *were hired* about the eleventh hour [5pm], they each received a denarius. But when the first came, they <u>supposed</u> that they would receive more; and they likewise received each a denarius" [*He began with a full day's wage— but they were freaked out...*] (Matthew 20:1-10, emphasis and brackets mine).

Why do we complain? The answer could be, in all honesty, because of a propensity to constantly compare ourselves with others. Why not look at the goodness and generosity of the Lord instead? Complaining makes you a target for engulfing strife and negativity.

"And when they had received *it,* **they complained against the landowner, saying, 'These last** *men* **have worked** *only* **one hour, and you made them equal to us who have borne the burden and the heat of the day.' But he answered one of them and said, 'Friend, I am doing you no wrong. Did you not agree with me for a denarius? Take** *what is* **yours and go your way. I wish to give to <u>this last man</u>** *the same* **as to you. Is it not lawful for me to do what I wish with my own things? Or is your eye evil [stingy] because I am good?' So the last will be first, and the first last. For many**

are called, but few chosen"' (Matthew 20:11-16, emphasis and brackets mine).

We may understand and sympathize, but didn't they agree (these ones from before 9am) to the working terms by going out to do the task?

As a side note, something similar happened with Israel at Sinai concerning the Law. They wanted to know the rule system so they could do it or try to 'keep it.'

"So Moses came and called for the elders of the people, and laid before them all these words which the LORD commanded him. Then all the people answered together and said, 'All that the

95

LORD has spoken we will do.' So Moses brought back the words of the people to the LORD" (Exodus 19:7-8).

"All that God commands, we can do it" they said. That sounds somewhat presumptuous. Then they received the Ten Commandments. They complained. They needed to see that they couldn't do it in their own power. God's strength flows through our weakness. In order to receive God's grace and generosity, we need to humble ourselves and see our need for a Savior. We must put aside all self-sufficiency and humbly recognize our need.

"For they did not gain possession of the land by their own sword, nor did their own arm save them; but it was Your right hand, Your arm, and the light of Your countenance, because You favored them" (Psalm 44:3, emphasis mine).

Anxiety and worry are just indicators that we're still self-righteous in those areas of our life that we're stressed about. As the verse said, **"So the last will be first, and the first last. For many are called, but few are chosen"** (Matthew 20:16). God desires to show His goodness, but He's challenging us to be among those who are **"chosen,"** meaning the ones who have developed a capacity of the heart to receive His abundant goodness.

Regarding the '100-fold' return coming to those who work in the kingdom, this parable reveals that all were called. The landowner—Jesus—went out to those from before 9am, at 9am, noon, 3pm, and 5pm. He didn't single anyone out, but gave the opportunity to them all. However, the ones who received were those who believed and were open for His generosity. Many are called but few are chosen. Who are chosen?

Those who will allow God to show them His goodness. Who gives Him the opportunity to show Himself 'Good.' Notice the phrase, "Whatever is right, I will <u>give to you</u>" (Matthew 20:4). What do you expect? God does not undervalue our work. He prizes our faith in Him and His Word! Personally, I believe we are the "evening" generation (see Matthew 20:8).

As believers in Christ, what are our motives for serving? The 9am group worked more, but went by faith. The noon group worked and went by faith too. Then later in the day, at both 3pm and 5pm, those workers went out too with the promise, "whatever is right I will give to you." As you observe the labor pool for the day, who do you think would be the most grateful? The 5pm group, for sure! They trusted and depended on the landowner, and He was generous to them. This gave them a revelation of God's grace and goodness even more than all the others!

"So the last will be first, and the first last. For many are called, but few chosen" (Matthew 20:16).

The landowner went out five times, which is the number of grace. The early group had an exacting term of agreement for the denarius (Matthew 20:2). Then the noon and 3pm groups were told, "whatever is right I will give to you" (Matthew 20:4-5). But the 5pm group—the evening generation, if you will—were told, "whatever is right, you will receive" (Matthew 20:7).

God has made promises to us. We are good receivers. Those of us upon whom the end of the ages have come have more knowledge of God, more revelation of grace, and have more of a capacity to be developed to expect a mighty harvest and abundance. We have developed a capacity of heart to receive God's abundance by knowing that "everything is already ours" (see Ephesians 1:3 & 2 Peter 1:3-4). This isn't selfish entitlement, but rather a revelation of the generosity of a good, good Father!

We need the ears to hear and the eyes to see—whoever is graced most, received most! So what do you see with your eyes closed? Do you expect restoration and help? Have you expanded your vision? Are you a good receiver? Is your posture one of receiving from God? Is your posture one of faith, expecting to receive of Him? I'm not appealing to your flesh and greed. I'm appealing to your born-again spirit and your soul's expectation to receive from God's goodness. Jesus was answering Peter's question. This parable was in response to a question!

No Envy

One of the life lessons I have seen, and been reminded of multiple times, from this parable is about the personal boundaries I see that I need to have in my life and relationships. As you can see from the Word, several of the workers were begrudging and envious of others they really had no right to resent because they were all just doing their jobs that they had agreed to do. You see, envy makes us resent people who have something we don't have. It feeds on itself, and is, ultimately, self-destructive. When we envy, the very people who are loving, safe, and generous become the bad guys in our eyes! Envy is best defined as a tendency to hate other people for having what we want. Envy says, "What is inside me is bad. What is outside me is good. I hate anyone who has something I desire." Except, we won't admit it's 'hate.'

Jesus taught about envy in this parable. Envy makes generosity sound unfair. It's the opposite of love, which **"does not envy...but rejoices in the truth"** (1 Corinthians 13:4, 6).

I learned clearly that envy is at the <u>ROOT</u> of betrayal! The chief priests had handed Jesus over to Pilate out of envy. They hated that He had more love inside of Him than they did...

> **"But Pilate answered them, saying, 'Do you want me to release to you the King of the Jews?' For he knew that the chief priests had handed Him over because of envy"** (Mark 15:9-10).

Because of envy, they wanted Jesus crucified and a murderous rebel released instead (Mark 15:11-15).

Here's What Happened

We have lived out our calling through walking by faith. After trying to sell our facility for over two long years, we now have a pending sale. Praise God! The Lord has been transitioning us, along with our congregation, and for us to go out more in ministry. After 25 years, we feel like it was the right time to sell the building and move to something more suitable for our church family with just one Celebration Service weekly and home groups meeting and throughout the week.

Our mortgage loan became due. We had a significant payoff amount. So we found a reputable Christian-based loan company that offered to obtain an additional amount to make repairs. After two months of jumping through every hoop and just two weeks before the loan was due for the refinance, we received a completely surprise call informing us they could not loan to us because of a doctrinal difference. To say that our hearts sunk would be an understatement. What a radical disappointment! Prayers of forgiveness are being offered even now. We knew that we couldn't react in desperation, but needed a word from God.

Right at this critical time, God gave me a dream of a ministry associate, and his face turned into the face of Donald Trump as he turned to look at me. Not knowing entirely what this meant, we reached out to him and asked for his help. He became the very expression of "The Negotiator!" This dear brother went to the banker on our behalf, and actually contacted the superior loan manager. Against all odds, he negotiated on the basis of our story and on our behalf. God miraculously gave us a six-month extension—just the right amount of time to refinance and sell the property. Upon the very day of our 25 year ministry anniversary celebration, we still didn't know officially whether we would lose the building and the equity. But actually, we did know in our hearts of God's faithful delivering power to meet us right where we were. So we were worshipping and trusting the Lord!

That very week, my husband (Dennis) spoke to the pastor's network that we serve as Regional Advocates for (Andrew Wommack's Association of Related Ministries International). He testified with passion and clarity of the delivering power of God in the middle of a raging storm. God brings us out so He can bring us in. He brings us into the land He has prepared for us, the land He has promised us! Just as in the parable of the workers in the vineyard—as part of the Evening Generation—let's expect to experience God's goodness and generosity too! Making a life application from the profoundly prophetic passage regarding the laborers in the vineyard, hasn't He said, "Whatever is right, you will receive"? Yes, Lord. We are good receivers!

Chapter 9

Shadow

With just one word, our minds can imagine a scene and paint a picture. In Jesus, there is a beautiful settled-ness in my soul of His constancy, knowing that...

"Every good gift and every perfect gift is from above, and comes down from the Father <u>of</u> lights, with whom there is <u>no</u> variation or <u>shadow of turning</u>" (James 1:17, emphasis mine).

God can be trusted. He doesn't shift and change in His relationship with us. The more I have grown in the true knowledge of the goodness of God, the more I have been relieved of fear, anxiety, and stress.

My newly-found brother (Kevin) was a man who came out of the shadows of living in his past into something new. He symbolizes and represents to me a restoration in progress.

Did you know that many Old Testament types and shadows, especially prophecies and prophetic Scriptures, have their fulfillment in the person of Jesus Christ? In the Word, we can receive revelation as something or someone "comes out of the shadows." That almost sounds spooky, as if something or someone is lurking in the dark fog. But I'm referring to leaving something behind and embracing the new. The word "shadow" means "a faint indication." When used as a verb, it means "to represent vaguely, mysteriously, or prophetically" (see American Heritage Dictionary). This is a call to come out of the shadows to live free from the shame and condemnation of your past.

Prisoner

"Then Jesus made a public spectacle of all the powers and principalities of darkness, stripping away from them every weapon and all their spiritual authority and power to accuse us. And by the power of the cross, Jesus led them around as prisoners in a procession of triumph. *He was not their prisoner; they were his!*" (Colossians 2:15 TPT).

As a young girl growing up in East St. Louis, Illinois, I heard my grandparents talk about my half-brother named Kevin. I had never met him, nor even knew his last name. Then when I was thirty, my sister found him. I finally came to know him, befriend him, help him, and—sadly—lose him in just a twenty-year span of time.

Kevin had been in a Texas maximum security prison almost all of his adult life. Being just two years apart in age, while I enjoyed a new marriage and raising children, he faced life as a young adult in a remote state penitentiary. We often create our own prisons—and they're in our minds! We shut ourselves behind bars of our own making. Jesus hands us the key to get out of prison, but we are the ONLY ONES who can use it to free ourselves. I can personally relate with this pain and sorrow in my own life and through my experience with my brother, Kevin. Many letters, prayers, and visits took place over decades. He received the redemption of his life.

This tall (6'6") handsome young man had a genuine encounter with the Lord during a near-death experience and miraculously met us at the very time when he had lost all hope of life. Led by the Holy Spirit, my sister researched and found him through family members she'd never met before. She contacted his mother, who reluctantly told her that Kevin was serving a life sentence in prison. Of course, meeting us impacted him deeply because of the kind of care and connection we had for him. He began looking at life with eyes of hope for a future. Raised as an only child, he suddenly discovered he had two half-sisters. He was enchanted with the whole idea. We were apprehensive, but very excited to get to know him.

For nearly six years, we made the long distance, quarterly visits to be with him before he was miraculously paroled after serving a life sentence. If you know anyone who has an incarcerated loved one, then you're aware of how much fear, guilt, and shame inmates struggle with. Life relationships and connections mean so much to them. Those that remain consistent through the trials and share God's unconditional love have the possibility of success. Through Christ, everyone has the ability to overcome all the odds stacked against them.

Kevin was very smart, had a charismatic personality, and was a friend to guards and other inmates alike. After receiving the Lord, he saw dozens and dozens of men come to Jesus through his witness and testimony of salvation. Upon parole, we were the ones he came to be with to launch his new life in a new state with a new slate.

Through the odd bond of relationship we shared, we watched him grow, gain meaningful relationships, and have a beautiful family. Yet, he still struggled so much because of the way he viewed himself. For me, all this was both joyous and miraculous, and difficult and painful at the same time. We went from the highest expectations for good things to the lowest of disappointments with bad choices Kevin made. His family—those closest to him—bore the scars of pain the most. Personally, I've overcome the trauma by giving it to God. I entrusted this to His care and am believing for His hand of restoration to work it out in the time to come. My brother won't come back on this earth, but His life mattered and the fulfillment of God's promises will continue for his daughters. It's all a fragile and sensitive scenario. I'm letting you in on our loss and disappointment—knowing you have yours too.

In America, the difficult truth regarding our prison system today is that those released early often go back again. Recidivism is a tendency to lapse into a previous pattern of behavior, especially a pattern of criminal habits. When you truly know all your sins are forgiven, you can relax. When you know you're loved, you can feel safe. This revelation coming from our relationship with God can trump contradicting feelings. The devil may shame and accuse, but Jesus gave us His approval and empowerment. Our willingness to renew our mind to the truth makes the difference of whether we experience God's best for us or not.

Killing Giants

If you fail to slay the giants in your path, they may kill you. Consider Goliath, the giant who harassed, accused, and condemned the armies of Israel. Young David asked...

> **"What's in it for the man who kills that Philistine and gets rid of this ugly blot on Israel's honor? Who does he think he is, anyway, this uncircumcised Philistine, taunting the armies of God-Alive?"** (1 Samuel 17:26 MSG).

Our victory truly lies in silencing the voice of accusation and condemnation by killing the giant in our minds! Slay the lying giant in your life with the truth of God's love and what His Word says you should believe about yourself. My brother Kevin lost his family—and ultimately his life here on earth—because of choices he made believing lies, even though God had better plans for him. You see, each and every one of us get to make the choice.

Before her untimely death, an interviewer asked pop singer Whitney Houston, "So which of the drugs was the demon for you? Crack? Cocaine? Heroin?" The famous diva looked at her for a moment, then answered, "None of them was the demon. I was, because I had the freedom to choose!"

Freedom from consequences doesn't mean you got by with something or that your freedom is free. We can never forget the cost of freedom. Just because God in His mercy has eradicated the consequences of my sin through His Son's costly sacrifice doesn't mean I should use that as an excuse to get worse. God forbid! In light of Jesus' death, burial, and resurrection, I choose to let Him enable me to get better! (see Romans 6; Galatians 5:1, 13; 1 Peter 2:16).

God blessed my brother Kevin, and I will reflect with joy on the miraculous story of coming to know him, and then the prayers being answered for his supernatural parole being—against all odds—granted. The Lord gave him many new relationships, including his wife (Grace) and their beautiful babies. We have our future throughout eternity to know one another. I have the connection with my sweet nieces, and see some of him in their eyes and mannerisms. I'm trusting God for continued restoration in all of our lives from the pain and chaos we went through together.

Reality Check

Kevin serves as an example of someone knowing 'about God' and His salvation, and experiencing something in a partial way. So much more was available to him and for him than what he actually stepped into. My brother wrestled with invisible pain and shame. He'd often cry as we spoke on the phone. I shared about God's unconditional love and the freedom the Lord wanted for him. Kevin's low self-worth remained so attached to his failed performance. He knew he had struck out at so many things that he was capable of accomplishing. He hadn't learned how to let go or forgive himself. He had no rest as he struggled to believe the truth about himself in Christ. One truth Kevin didn't realize was that the enemy was defeated and had no power over him, except that which he deceived him into believing.

The truth and reality from the Word of God—the substance, what was foreshadowed in the Old Testament—the body of it belongs to Christ!

"[God] disarmed the principalities and powers that were ranged against us and made a bold display *and* public example of them, in triumphing over them in Him *and* in it [the cross]. Therefore let no one sit in judgment on you in matters of food and drink, or with regard to a feast day or a New Moon or a Sabbath. Such [things] are only the <u>shadow</u> of things that are to come, *and* they have only a symbolic value. But the reality (the substance, the solid fact of what is foreshadowed, the body of it) belongs to Christ" (Colossians 2:15-17 AMPC, emphasis mine).

This passage speaks so clearly of an overcoming accomplishment through the Cross. Then it instructs believers not to allow themselves to be scrutinized or judged by rule-keepers (legalists) in matters that were actually painting a picture of something to come that also culminated in Jesus. Each of these things listed in verse 16 served to represent something that Messiah would accomplish. Now that Jesus the Messiah has come, the representation isn't necessary.

A Shadow from Around the Corner

"These are a shadow of the things that were to come; the reality, however, is found in Christ" (Colossians 2:17 NIV).

A shadow is never as important as the person who casts it. Those who cling to the Old Testament shadow are missing the New Testament reality found in Jesus. So this verse gives us a reality check.

Christ is the body who cast all the Old Testament shadows. Now that we have Jesus Himself, why would anyone still cling to the shadow? In this passage, Paul revealed that these things were 'shadows of things to come.' Why keep hammering this point? Because throughout the modern church today, many believers have clung to the old system—the Old Covenant. Yet, we cannot mix the covenants!

If I were walking toward you, but the corner of a building blocked your view,

106

then my shadow could be very significant. It could show you that I was coming and how close I was, but once I came around the corner into full view, it would be unthinkable for you to fall down and embrace my shadow. My shadow is meaningful only because it represents me. Once you could talk to me straightaway, my shadow would be meaningless.

Old Testament rituals were significant before Christ came, illustrating truths that were not yet in full view. But now that Christ has come, the rituals are meaningless and can be oppressive if they are wrongfully thought to be requirements for acceptance by God (see Life for Today Commentary notes by Andrew Wommack).

Jesus Christ is the body who cast all the Old Testament shadows. Now that we have Jesus Himself, why would anyone still cling to the shadow? What is the 'shadow of things to come'? Remember, the word 'shadow' means 'a faint indication.' Anyone who uses the Old Testament dietary laws for anything other than symbolism that finds its complete fulfillment in Christ is in error. Those who preach that the dietary laws were for health reasons are missing the point that Paul was making in these verses. While writing Timothy, he even clarified saying that **"forbidding to eat meat"** is a doctrine of devils (1 Timothy 4:1-3). Yikes!

Christ Reality

"So don't let anyone condemn you for what you eat or drink, or for not celebrating certain holy days or new moon ceremonies or Sabbaths. For these rules are only shadows of the reality yet to come. And Christ himself is that reality. Don't let anyone condemn you by insisting on pious self-denial or the worship of angels, saying they have had visions about these things. Their sinful minds have made them proud, and they are not connected to Christ, the head of the body. For he holds the whole body together

107

with its joints and ligaments, and it grows as God nourishes it" (Colossians 2:16-19 NLT).

I think of our elaborate rule-keeping systems—and prison life is an example of one form of them. It's a system set up for failure. Once people are in the system, they often begin a downward spiral of not being able to jump through the hoops. The truth is that the loving support of a friend could undergird their ability to overcome. That's what Jesus did by fulfilling the laws and rules. Now we have the relationship!

As you look for a friend coming to meet you for lunch, you might get excited to see his shadow approaching, but you would be crazy to run up to him and hug his shadow! Once he rounds the corner and you see him in person—that's all that matters. It's a relationship! A shadow is never as important as the person who casts it. Those who cling to the Old Testament shadow are missing the New Testament reality found in Jesus.

As it stands, so many believers have missed the point. We all need to grasp the understanding that true self-denial as the Scriptures promote is not self-hatred or masochism, but rather an enthroning of Christ above self. We have a new identity in Christ that replaces the 'old self.' This isn't done in order to obtain salvation but as a response of love to what Christ has already done for us. He gave His all for us, and we willingly give our all back to Him. Self-denial as an attempt to earn salvation is always motivated by guilt and characterized by rigid rules, as Paul described in this passage. We can come out of the shadows of the past and let them go, recognizing that the true shadow has been cast in Jesus. Everything from the Old Testament that pointed to Him is now fulfilled in Jesus Christ. How I wish this profound truth could be more understood by the body of Christ! How many more people would live in freedom? No returns to prison. The prison door is open and it's time to go free. Believe the truth in your heart, not your head (see Life for Today notes by Andrew Wommack).

Chapter 10
Mountains

Stay fixed on Jesus! He's the center of the universe—we are not. He is fixed upon us!

As I have driven through the mountains so many times, the magnitude and grandeur of them always diminishes the size of homes, cars, and people. We are so seemingly small in the expanse and vastness of the landscape. While God keeps His eye on us and declares our value, dignity, and worth, it's so important to keep in mind that the universe revolves around Him. Yet, we are the apple of His eye! (see Psalm 17:8)

As I grew in the simple truth that God loves us and has laid His own life down for us, I would often ask Him in the quietness of my devotions, "Lord, do You really feel this way about me, or are you patronizing me?" I wasn't trying to be glib or disrespectful, but in my suspicious thinking I found it hard to grasp the proportion of His love for me—even as I was perceiving it.

"For by Him all things were created that are in heaven and that are on earth, visible and invisible, whether thrones or dominions or

principalities or powers. All things were created through Him and for Him" (Colossians 1:16).

Colorado

Even though they're all over our country in different places, when I think of mountains I first think of them in Colorado. God has divinely connected our lives with Colorado from the beginning of our marriage. Many of our closest relationships have been with so many friends from there. We took one of our first skiing vacations there five years after being married.

We've traveled back and forth from our home in Kansas City countless times on trips to Colorado. Both the headquarters of Andrew Wommack Ministries (Woodland Park) and also Faith Ministries International Network (Denver) are located there. We've been to annual ministers' conferences for decades and have benefited by sitting under the teaching and training of many great men and women of God.

For fourteen years our local church in Kansas City discipled us, but it wasn't until we heard the 'life altering good-news gospel message' through Andrew Wommack that our lives took a radical shift. Andrew & Jamie have had a passion to serve ministry leaders in the body of Christ, and have done so faithfully over the years from humble beginnings and in the most excellent of ways. The high point for us has been how the wisdom of God was imparted to us through these men and women. It helped ease some of the difficulties and hardships that ministers go through, adding such depth to our lives relationally. Andrew Wommack has dedicated his life to teaching and fulfilling God's call. Through his relationship with the Lord, faith, and obedience, he's carrying the revelation and mandate to impact the world with the good news gospel. We are honored to have known him from his beginning days in ministry and delight to see the expansion of the vision being fulfilled in our lifetime!

For two decades, we've worked with Dave & Bonnie Duell—pastors, apostles, and founders of Faith Ministries International Network. Both their teaching and mentoring impacted us in such a deep and personal way. Their relational leadership style—and emotional and spiritual support—influenced us as young pastors. Their patient loving example freed us to be who God created us to be. We had the great privilege of traveling with Dave & Bonnie for the last twenty years. Together, we hosted conferences, launched ministries, and took missions teams to nations all over the world. Dave operated strongly in gifts of faith, healings, and workings of miracles. He flowed in the prophetic joyfully and oozed the love of God the Father to all. His beloved wife—Bonnie—has such an exceptional ability to teach and administrate. We shared in a bond of friendship, shopping, and similar gifting. When we can team up with other like-minded leaders to collaborate in the kingdom of God, the whole body of Christ benefits!

Our lives have been lived visiting churches, meeting leaders, transporting training materials, launching ministries, starting Bible schools, having short-term medical clinics, and doing outreaches. Through God's empowerment, the spread of the message of God's goodness and grace has multiplied countless times over. We have seen a demonstration of the Holy Spirit's power in life-changing ways! Individual lives were transformed, healed, and released from oppressions and fears. We are who we are today because of our relationships with these wonderful people.

Thus, the mountains mean something magnificent to me in various ways. His creation speaks of Him...

> **"Yet for us there is but one God, the Father, who is the source of all things, and we *exist* for Him; and one Lord, Jesus Christ, by whom are all things [that have been created], and we [believers exist and have life and have been redeemed] through Him"** (1 Corinthians 8:6 AMP).

Viewing mountain ranges has enlarged my perspective of the size and scope of God's greatness.

Moving Mountains

When we think of mountains, we also often think of overcoming insurmountable obstacles. In our stand of faith, we SPEAK to problems to move (see Mark 11:22-24). Faith in God sees with the eyes of our heart. With our heart believing in God's 'bigness,' we can command the mountainous problems to diminish or 'move.' That could even be longstanding family issues through the generations. I have often taught about faith in God and the displacement of big problems through trusting in Him and our authority in Christ.

When I think of mountains, I also think of the covenants—especially the old and the new. Have you seen the movie *The Ten Commandments*? It's a must-see! In Scripture, mountains can represent the Old and New Covenants. You need to become familiar with the whole story of Moses on Mount Sinai and the giving of the Ten Commandments (see Exodus 19 & 20). But remember, the people were afraid of God's presence. That's not the way for us to live.

> **"Now all the people witnessed the thunderings, the lightning flashes, the sound of the trumpet, and the mountain smoking; and when the people saw *it,* they trembled and stood afar off. Then they said to Moses, 'You speak with us, and we will hear; but let not God speak with us, lest we die'"** (Exodus 20:18- 19).

The author of the book of Hebrews lays out for us quite a contrast to this for today. It's such a dramatic picture painted for us that it should forever change the way we see what belongs to us in Jesus. Imagine if this were the scene from a movie—ominous and scary. The music might be sinister piano chords—eerie, creepy, and creating an expectation for the mysterious...

112

Mount Sinai Vs. Mount Zion

Moses went up the mountain at the giving of the Law…

"Unlike your ancestors, <u>you didn't come to Mount Sinai</u>—all that volcanic blaze and earthshaking rumble—to hear God speak. The earsplitting words and soul- shaking message terrified them and they begged him to stop. When they heard the words—'If an animal touches the Mountain, it's as good as dead'—they were afraid to move. Even Moses was terrified. No, that's not *your* experience at all. <u>You've come to Mount Zion</u>, the city where the living God resides. The invisible Jerusalem is populated by throngs of festive angels and Christian citizens. It is the city where God is Judge, with judgments that make us just. You've come to Jesus, who presents us with a new covenant, a fresh charter from God. He is the Mediator of this covenant. The murder of Jesus, unlike Abel's—a homicide that cried out for vengeance—became a proclamation of grace. So don't turn a deaf ear to these gracious words. If those who ignored earthly warnings didn't get away with it, what will happen to us if we turn our backs on heavenly warnings? His voice that time shook the earth to its foundations; this time—he's told us this quite plainly—he'll also rock the heavens: 'One last shaking, from top to bottom, stem to stern.' The phrase 'one last shaking' means a thorough housecleaning, getting rid of all the historical and religious junk so that the unshakable essentials stand clear and uncluttered. <u>Do you see what we've got?</u> <u>An unshakable kingdom</u>! And do you see how thankful we must be? Not only thankful, but brimming with worship, deeply reverent before God. For God is not an indifferent bystander. He's

113

actively cleaning house, torching all that needs to burn, and he won't quit until it's all cleansed. God himself is Fire!" (Hebrews 12:18-29 MSG, emphasis mine).

Notice how this passage completely locates us—where we are and where we're not! We have *not* come to Mount Sinai. This proclamation of grace is our banner. We cannot afford to ignore it. We can't hold to the religious trappings all around us. So many of us hold on to the works-based religion like a trunk of a tree. Hey, the fruit grows out on the limb. We have come to Mount Zion! But when the shaking happens all around us, we'll be rattled to our core and fall out of it to the ground. It won't work for us. You already know too much. He knows you, and you have already begun to encounter and experience His great love. Besides, all our dead works will burn.

Whole Lotta Shaking Going On

"See that you do not refuse Him who speaks. For if they did not escape who refused Him who spoke on earth, much more *shall we not escape* if we turn away from Him who *speaks* from heaven, whose voice then shook the earth; but now He has promised, saying, 'Yet once more I shake not only the earth, but also heaven.' Now this, 'Yet once more,' indicates the removal of those things that are being shaken, as of things that are made, that the things which cannot be shaken may remain. Therefore, since we are receiving a kingdom which cannot be shaken, let us have grace, by which we may serve God acceptably with reverence and godly fear. For our God *is* a consuming fire" (Hebrews 12:25-29).

See that you do not reject or disregard Him that speaks. That is, the gospel. Don't refuse the good news gospel being spoken to you. Don't refuse the covenant offered through Mount Zion.

"You've come to Jesus, who presents us with a new covenant, a

114

fresh charter from God. He is the Mediator of this covenant" (Hebrews 12:24 MSG).

Spend time meditating on this passage. It will revolutionize your thinking and transform your soul. This kingdom cannot be shaken. He tells us **"let us have grace"** because by it we'll serve God acceptably with reverential awe (Hebrews 12:28). In essence, "You may have refused to hear Him then, but don't refuse to hear Him now. You have come to Mount Zion, the refuge of His mercy." What a contrast between the people's terrified approach to God at Mount Sinai and their approach at Mount Zion. Before Jesus came, God seemed distant and threatening. After Jesus came, God welcomes us through Christ into His very presence even where angels celebrate.

The difficulty with the Old Testament Law was you couldn't keep it, and in your attempt to do so it was all about you looking at yourself. In our New Covenant, it's all about you seeing JESUS Who fulfilled it.

The gospel is speaking! The Word made flesh—Jesus—is speaking. Grace is a person. This is how you'll live out your destiny blueprint. Acknowledging Him and His empowering presence on the inside of you will cause your purpose to emerge. Do not turn away from Him Who has addressed you in this new dispensation, and called you to obey and serve Him.

God had addressed them in the gospel as surely as He had addressed the Hebrews on Mount Sinai. There's much to be dreaded in disregarding His voice now, as there was then. He spoke then (Mount Sinai) amidst lightening, thunder, and clouds, but now by the Holy Spirit and all His calls and warnings in the gospel (see Hebrews 1:2).

According to verse 25, those who heard God under the old dispensation, and refused to obey Him, were cut off—Moses being the spokesperson. The contrast in this passage is between Moses and Jesus. Moses, a mere man, spoke in the name of God. Jesus, the Son of God, spoke as from heaven.

Hebrews 12:26-27 speaks of shaking, which quotes in part...

115

"For thus says the LORD of hosts: 'Once more (it *is* a little while) I will shake heaven and earth, the sea and dry land; and I will shake all nations, and they shall come to the Desire of All Nations, and I will fill this temple with glory,' says the LORD of hosts" (Haggai 2:6-7).

Haggai prophesied the changes that would take place under the Messiah. This means there would be <u>great revolutions</u> at His coming, as if the universe were shaken to its center. The writer of Hebrews applies this passage to the first coming of Jesus, our Redeemer. Emphasis is laid on the fact that not only the *earth* was to be shaken, but also *heaven*. The shaking of the earth here evidently refers to the commotions among the nations that would prepare the way for the coming of the Messiah.

An Unshakable Kingdom

The ominous music is still playing… Think of this grandiose summation: The meaning of the whole then is, that while the giving of the Law at Mount Sinai, fearful and solemn as it was, was an event that merely shook the earth in the vicinity of the holy Mount, the introduction <u>of the gospel agitated the whole universe</u>. The introduction of the gospel was a much more solemn and momentous event than the giving of the Law!

Verse 28 continues, **"Let us have grace, by which we may serve God"** meaning "let us hold fast the grace or favor which we have received in being admitted to the privileges of that kingdom." The writer's goal is to keep them in the reverent fear and service of God. The argument presented is that this kingdom is permanent. There's no danger of its being overthrown. It's unshakable!

All Creation Groans

Talk about some heavy-duty insights into these passages of Scripture! Once we see them, we'll become settled in the simplicity of this revelation.

"**For I consider that the sufferings of this present time are not worthy *to be compared* with the glory which shall be revealed <u>in us</u>.**" (Romans 8:18, emphasis mine).

This is a very important statement. Paul did not say that this glory would be revealed "to us" but rather "in us."

"**For the <u>earnest expectation</u> of the creation eagerly waits for the revealing of the sons of God**" (Romans 8:19, emphasis mine).

"**Earnest expectation**" means "intense anticipation" or "to strain forward" or literally "await with outstretched head." It's a turning away from all other things and concentration on a single object (see Life for Today notes by Andrew Wommack).

"**For I consider that the sufferings of this present time are not worthy *to be compared* with the glory which shall be revealed <u>in us</u>. For the earnest expectation of the creation eagerly waits for the revealing of the sons of God. For the creation was subjected to futility, not willingly, but because of Him who subjected *it* in hope; because the creation itself also will be delivered from the bondage of corruption into the glorious liberty of the children of God. For we know <u>that the whole creation groans and labors with birth pangs together until now</u>. Not only *that,* but we also who have the first fruits of the Spirit, even we ourselves groan within ourselves, eagerly waiting for the adoption, the redemption of our body. For we were saved in this hope, but hope that is seen is not hope; for why does one still hope for what he sees? But if we hope for what we do not see, we eagerly wait for *it* with perseverance. Likewise the Spirit also helps in our weaknesses. For we do not know what** we should pray for as we ought, but the Spirit Himself makes intercession for us with groanings which cannot be uttered. Now He who searches the hearts knows what the mind of the Spirit *is*, because He makes intercession for the saints according to *the will of* God. And we know that all things work together for good to those who love God, to those who are the called according to *His* purpose" (Romans 8:18-28, emphasis mine).

The whole creation longingly waits for you to RELEASE what you have in Christ. Even the animal kingdom and nature waits to see us release what's in us. Verse 19 makes it very clear that the whole creation is eagerly and intensely anticipating the day when the glory of God that is already deposited within God's saints will be revealed. Even now creation rejoices every time some saint manifests His glory here on this earth.

You cannot manifest something that does not already exist…

"Beloved, now we are children of God; and it has not yet been revealed what we shall be…" (1 John 3:2).

We are already the sons of God. This isn't something that has yet to transpire. The whole creation is waiting for us to manifest what is already in us. I believe that through our revelation of His unshakable kingdom, His promises to us, and His Spirit living through us we will manifest the mountain-moving faith that started as only a mustard seed.

For the past twenty-five years, the Lord took our lives and our spiritual connections with ministry associates from the mountains of Colorado to further expound the greatest revelation in our lives regarding the two mountains— Mount Sinai and Mount Zion. Let us have grace whereby we may serve God! It's time to manifest what is already within us. We can live out our destiny in this unshakable kingdom!

Chapter 11

Oceans

Rest is a weapon from God, and we use weapons against an enemy. The enemy of our soul hates our position of rest in Christ because he wants us stressed and overly preoccupied, never experiencing what has been done for us. Now, clearly different people mean very different things when we speak of the 'rest' in God. This isn't rest as in 'napping' because you are tired. Rest in God has to do with what you believe about God and what He has already done for us through His birth, death, burial, and resurrection.

Thus far, I've tried to give you a glimpse—from many different angles—of the rest we have in Christ's finished work. From God's Word being rooted in your heart and bringing about an effortless transformation to putting your robe of righteousness on by believing and allowing the true identity of Christ to be your self-image. Then I challenged you to rest in the fact that you grow and mature from babyhood by believing in your right standing with God and allowing your faith to be stable in that truth.

Rest in Christ—not the latest pillow-top mattress—brings you into great confidence in Christ's accomplishment on your behalf. You are Christ's heir of promise by believing. I shared about inheritance and lands that the Lord has faithfully led us into in our life and ministry. God is interested in us personally, and not just what we do for Him!

Shadows of the past will try to loom over and steal what God is doing in the present and future through broken-heartedness and disappointment. We all face it, walk through it, grieve over it, and—hopefully—choose to let that go. The real 'shadow' is the one depicted in the Old Testament, which all point to Christ and show us what's to come in our relationship with Jesus. Everything fulfilled in Him is now ours. When we find ourselves hidden in Christ, and rest in that relationship, striving to please or earn anything from Him ceases.

The mountains mean so much to me, not just all the significant life connections and refreshing time spent in the Rockies, but also the ever-so-powerful Mount Zion. It's where the gospel of peace resounded to agitate the universe. The Word was given, declared by a Voice we cannot refute so that in resting (or believing) we inherit the unshakable kingdom (see Hebrews 12:25, 28).

Most everyone loves the thought of vacationing at a beach, including me. If I'm going on a vacay, whether on a Caribbean cruise or to an all-inclusive resort, I know it's time to relax. Unwinding and letting go of built up life tensions is a natural byproduct of a getaway weekend of sunshine and saltwater.

At certain times in my childhood, I went to Tampa Bay where my grandmother lived. We'd wake up before sunrise while it was still dark out, pack a breakfast to eat, and then walk over on the bayshore. She'd drink her black coffee from a thermos while we enjoyed a bacon and egg sandwich watching the sunrise over the water. Reflecting on this childhood memory has helped bring me more into God's rest and promise. Trusting God has a posture. Receiving His goodness sounds like praising Him before you see it. I've always had a special love for the beach. Being seaside contains a lot of symbolic meaning for me. We all need to find the 'happy place' where it's easiest for us to connect with the Lord and quiet our soul (mind, will, & emotions) to encounter Him.

Experiencing the love of God through meditating on His promises facilitates expanding the capacity of our heart to receive God's best. His Word reveals His true nature and imparts hope to us. We have to intentionally dismiss the thoughts and ideas that counter the truth about Him in some of our negative life experiences. We may have felt God let us down, but reality check: He's not the one to blame for the stuff that happens in a fallen world where we have been given power and authority. Remember, we are joint heirs with Christ.

A reflection as simple as the constancy of ocean waves and tides washing up day after day serve as a continual reminder of God cleansing away our past. His serenity assures us of His love on the swell of every foaming surf coming in to shore.

Making a Move

My daughter (Alison) asked me if I'd consider coming out to the East Coast where she had recently moved. Of course, that was a great getaway. When I arrived, she began asking if we'd consider investing in a vacation rental property. It seemed like such a far-out thought with all the logistics and expenses that would have to work out. She had been going through so much in her life, including difficulties with divorce and her unsettled job situation. We'd wanted to be supportive of her with this new move and we missed her so much.

My husband and I discussed this possibility while lying in bed one night. I really wondered about taking her up on her suggestion. That was a deep desire within my heart. I'd never even fully entertained such a thing before because the possibility of a dream like that being fulfilled was so remote. Yet, within a few weeks of that conversation, while my husband rode around on a scooter in our neighborhood, a total stranger randomly approached and asked him if anyone in our subdivision was selling their home. What?!?

Well, we had custom designed and built our English Tudor cottage home of thirty years. This was no small decision for us! We had great emotional attachments to this charming customized home we had built in the woods, including all the memories of raising our family there. Yet, we were willing for more adventure in what God had for us. Opening up our hearts was a stretch and a step of faith! God amazed us, showed us His incredible ways, and met us right where we were at. We further discussed that possibility with the set of conditions we wanted to be met, the price we desired, and the next steps of where to move locally. We received a phone call back from this young family man that he was willing to meet our terms.

We never even had the challenge of finding a realtor, staging our house, or hosting showings so people could come through and see it. Instead, the need was instantaneously met through this divine connection and this family giving us our exact asking price. Within thirty days we had closed the sale and loaded moving pods that took half of our belongings to North Carolina and the other half to our new apartment locally.

Our daughter Ali, and new son-in-law, Nick found multiple island houses for us to view online. We took a few days and poured over lovely beach homes with views and sounds of swashing breakers. They made their suggestions. We made our decision and closed that deal too, thanking God for His attentive help in finding this house!

This happening developed through a growing relationship with Jesus and from an expanding lifetime revelation of walking in an expectation of good from Him. Over time, the capacity of my heart to receive gifts from God has been increasing without strange concepts of feeling undeserving or guilty. It's simply Him showing the reality of His goodness to me without me feeling ashamed to tell about it. That may be a foreign concept to many people, while others can totally relate. It has come in a way that brings restoration to my formerly broken heart and damaged soul (from life's disappointments). So I am ocean-side once again! God gave us a beach house. It's our vacation rental property and place to share with friends and family.

The waves rolling in onto the shore are filled with tangible evidence of God's unconditional love for me. His voice speaks through the sea sprays and their never ending crashes onto dry land, which reveal…

> **"Mightier than the thunder of the great waters, mightier than the breakers of the sea—the LORD on high is mighty"** (Psalm 93:4 NIV).

Working behind the Scenes

This meaningful transition time in my life has marked my heart with an awareness of God's bigger plan. He brought dreams and desires to pass. I opened up to His desire to do it for me through knowing His generous ways—and I know there is more to come! As I write this today, I'm going from the East Coast to the West Coast with the same message and revelation of God's faithfulness to fulfill the desires of our heart. He's the One Who actually put them there! (see Psalm 37:4). For me, 'seaside' is the equivalent of experiencing God's rest—believing in what He has done and is doing for us. A healthy relationship is rooted in acceptance that diminishes striving and having to prove something.

Sometimes overworking can become your validation and identity. We may think, *Look at me God, and all I've done for You. Now You owe me!* This is just one more performance trap. But our Father and Friend wants us to know that things are already in motion on our behalf. He's working things out behind the scenes. We don't have to earn it…

> **"But by the grace of God I am what I am, and His grace toward me was not in vain; but I labored more abundantly than they all, yet not I, but the grace of God** *which was* **with me"** (1 Corinthians 15:10).

Paul acknowledged God's grace as the source of everything he had and was, but he allowed God's grace to have its full effect in his life through seeking God more than the other apostles did. We have to labor against the flesh to rest in God's grace (see Hebrews 4:11; Life for Today Commentary by Andrew Wommack). We rest and depend upon God's ability at work in our lives. Wherever we are weak, we can draw upon His strength. Paul had a strong work ethic, but his confidence wasn't in himself. We can rest in Christ's finished work that same way. The **only** time we are ever admonished to:

> *"let us fear lest any of you seem to have come short of it."* (Hebrews 4:1)

That's quite a warning! But why? Because of the serious and damaging consequences of NOT grasping what has already been done for you.

Days of Heaven on Earth

I'm learning to freely receive and expect good things from God because He loves me. We reflect on God's Word and look at the essence and intention from Him toward us. Even back in the Old Testament book of Deuteronomy, God says...

> **"Therefore you shall lay up these words of mine in your heart and in your soul, and bind them as a sign on your hand, and they shall be as frontlets between your eyes. You shall teach them to your children, speaking of them when you sit in your house, when you walk by the way, when you lie down, and when you rise up. And you shall write them on the doorposts of your house and on your gates, that your days and the days of your children may be multiplied in the land of which the LORD swore to your fathers to give them, <u>like the days of the heavens above the earth</u>"** (Deuteronomy 11:18-21, emphasis mine).

124

We can trust God for these kinds of days. One can choose to be restored from disillusionment, disappointment, and sorrow. We can expect restoration! God recently spoke a promise to me regarding something He was doing through me from 'coast to coast.' While working on this chapter, I sat in the fulfillment of it on the West Coast as I then traveled to the East Coast. God declares that He will cause what has 'been' to become His oasis of love. His water will become even more powerful as a fountain that shoots up forceful water of His Spirit. God says, "When you rest in Me, I work. And when you work, I rest."

We can only give away what we have received. Our lives are the training ground for true ministry. Enjoy it as you can. Actually, every believer is a minister because of the Life-Giver being in us. Ministry truly is a product of who you are, not what you do! We are big advocates for preparation and Bible training after knowing God's calling. We had a Life Bible Training School, taught in it, and equipped believers in our local church ministry for more than fifteen years. Our graduates have been launched into business and ministry and are fulfilling purpose and vision. Live life with great expectation!

Resting in God is a weapon. It's spiritual warfare—resting—to receive the fulfillment of His promise to you. We are complete in Christ! That's real faith-that's real believing.

Chapter 12
Rivers

Do you thirst? Good! Living water is available...

> **"On the last day, that great *day* of the feast, Jesus stood and cried out, saying, 'If anyone thirsts, let him come to Me and drink. He who believes in Me, as the Scripture has said, <u>out of his heart will flow rivers of living water</u>.' But this He spoke concerning the Spirit, whom those believing in Him would receive; for the Holy Spirit was not yet *given,* because Jesus was not yet glorified"** (John 7:37-39, emphasis mine).

Rivers of living water! As we allow God to fill us with His Spirit, we are capable of the rivers of release as we let go of hurts, wounds, pain, and betrayal. Be filled with His Spirit and be empowered to release. It's a flow, so let it go!

"Born to be wild..." Can you hear it now? Our lives are meant for purpose and adventure in what God has in store for us. Early in my walk with Jesus, I had to deal with deep roots of unforgiveness and disappointment. Like the movie character 'Bob', I had to take 'baby steps' to progress in life and improve my mental and emotional health. The ministry of the Holy Spirit in our lives coupled with our willingness to love and forgive others will cause us to be unstoppable!

True Forgiveness—The Heart of the Gospel

The first order of the journey of coming out of a dysfunctional and hurtful past is to really let go of the pain of our baggage and allow the Holy Spirit to help us to truly forgive ourselves and others. I remember holding grudges and resentment, as if I kept a blacklist. The Lord showed me how to choose forgiveness and release others and myself.

We have a perfected spirit man, and are born to be WILD in the kingdom of God! His seed in us gives birth to God-plans! He has created us for exploits (see Daniel 11:32; John 14:12). Why isn't the body of Christ living in the victory God intended for us?

One of my favorite Old Testament prophecies, which is so often quoted, but completely out of context, says…

> **"For My thoughts *are* not your thoughts, nor *are* your ways My ways," says the LORD. For *as* the heavens are higher than the earth, so are My ways higher than your ways, and My thoughts than your thoughts. For as the rain comes down, and the snow from heaven, and do not return there, but water the earth, and make it bring forth and bud, that it may give seed to the sower and bread to the eater, so shall My word be that goes forth from My mouth; it shall not return to Me void, but it shall accomplish what I please, and it shall prosper *in the thing* for which I sent it"** (Isaiah 55:8-11).

The context of this passage is about God's pardoning, as communicated in the verse immediately before…

> **"Let the wicked forsake his way, and the unrighteous man his thoughts; let him return to the LORD, and He will have mercy on him; and to our God, for He will abundantly pardon"** (Isaiah 55:7).

God's forgiveness is such that He abundantly pardons, which is why His ways are not our ways. We want to be people who operate in God's ways, so we need to be people who abundantly pardon. We must be willing to be abundantly pardoned!

Taking verses 8-11, apart from the context of verse 7, people often quote this passage as if to say that God is so elusive and mystical—we cannot understand Him. But keeping in mind the context of verse 7 throws a whole different light on the passage. The REASON God's thoughts are higher than ours is because He's so forgiving!

Born of God

"For this is the love of God, that we keep His commandments. And His commandments are not burdensome. For whatever is born of God overcomes the world. And this is the victory that has overcome the world—our faith. Who is he who overcomes the world, but he who believes that Jesus is the Son of God?" (1 John 5:3-5).

"Whoever has been born of God does not sin, for His seed remains in him; and <u>he cannot sin, because he has been born of God</u>" (1 John 3:9, emphasis mine).

Did you see that? He cannot sin because he has been born of God. We have a perfected spirit man. God's seed in us is giving birth to His plans. We are born to be wild in the kingdom of God!

Babies grow inside their mothers without a decision on their part about their own birth. They come forth in the fullness of time. That's a mini-picture of how things come to fruition in our lives. Destinies emerge with the surrounding conditions playing a factor in it all.

Release & Forgive

It's not about us earning or getting anything from God. If you need a healing, the Bible says you HAVE a healing. If you need a miracle, the Miracle-Worker lives inside of you. It's not so much about us getting anything from God, but about releasing things that weigh us down, or erroneous belief systems. A person gets used to living with weights, limited thinking, but we can choose to release some of the things that are hindering us from experiencing the victory that Jesus won for us. In fact, we need to guard the place of peace and rest!

My prayer is that with each chapter, you are doing heart work—allowing the truth to change your inner belief system. Then there's an eradicating of our self-sufficient and self-righteous attitudes that we've adopted in our religiosity. Sometimes we can deceive ourselves. We realize through our relationship with our Father that His secrets are revealed to us. We discover and know our identity and image as His sons and daughters.

In order to obey God and do what He commissions us to do, we need to hear the still, small voice from within cheering us on and pay attention to what's going on in our heart. It is in the solitude of a knowing assurance that we hear the voice of God. When we guard and protect creativity within from a place of peace and rest, we function best and become super-creative. Jesus called us to a place of safety and acceptance in Him. Jesus is, after all, the 'Prince of Peace.' Where the Lord is present, there will be peace.

Where We Function Best

The power of forgiveness is clearly revealed in the story after Jesus' resurrection. It's the universal crux of the good news gospel…

"Mary Magdalene went, telling the news to the disciples: 'I saw the Master!' And she told them everything he said to her. Later on that day, the disciples had gathered together, but, fearful of the Jews, had locked all the doors in the house. Jesus entered, stood among them, and said, 'Peace to you.' Then he showed them his hands and side. The disciples, seeing the Master with their own eyes, were exuberant. Jesus repeated his greeting: 'Peace to you.

129

Just as the Father sent me, I send you.' Then he took a deep breath and breathed into them. 'Receive the Holy Spirit,' he said. 'If you forgive someone's sins, they're gone for good. If you don't forgive sins, what are you going to do with them?'" (John 20:18-23 MSG, emphasis mine).

We have a choice to either hold on to someone's sins or let them go—but not as if we're stepping into the place of God. When you know someone has something against you, you can often sense it when you walk into a room. It's as if Jesus was saying, "Peace (a welcome greeting) I'm sending you, receive the Holy Spirit, and you need Him so you can release things through forgiving" (too often we retain our judgments against others).

Many people look at these verses in John 20 as the birth of the Church. We know on the day of Pentecost, the disciples were all empowered (see Acts 1 & 2). But this is an awesome saying: The Lord was giving the disciples a commission. Considering closely the order in which Christ spoke these things, it shows that the heart of the gospel is in the power of forgiveness. We have been forgiven and we can extend forgiveness to others, or choose not to. This is upside-down of how this world works!

Our experience confirms that no matter how far along you get in God, offenses will come—and often on a daily basis. Jesus warned us about this...

> "Then He said to the disciples, 'It is impossible that no offenses should come, but woe *to him* through whom they do come! It would be better for him if a millstone were hung around his neck, and he were thrown into the sea, than that he should offend one of these little ones. Take heed to yourselves. If your brother sins against you, rebuke him; and if he repents, forgive him. And if he sins against you seven times in a day, and seven times in a day returns to you, saying, 'I repent,' you shall forgive him'" (Luke 17:1-4, emphasis mine).

We must take responsibility with how we deal with offenses when they come to us. Jesus said we are to forgive 70 x 7...

> **"Then Peter came to Him and said, 'Lord, how often shall my brother sin against me, and I forgive him? Up to seven times?' Jesus said to him, 'I do not say to you, up to seven times, but up to seventy times seven'"** (Matthew 18:21- 22).

It's interesting that the disciples asked for an increase of faith in the area of releasing and forgiving people, and not in any other area...

> **"And the apostles said to the Lord, 'Increase our faith'"** (Luke 17:5).

It takes God's grace to be able to release people! Because offenses can come on a daily basis, it can cause us to stumble and hinder our operating in our calling.

What Forgiveness Is Not

It's not approval of what just occurred. Jesus forgave the woman caught in adultery, but it didn't mean He approved of her sin (see John 8:1-11).

It's not excusing. Why do we do that? We don't forgive someone; we just excuse them to make it easier for us to forgive.

It's not condoning or pardoning. This is a legal term meaning, 'to release from consequences.' Jesus is the only One who can release us from consequences. We don't have the power to release someone from consequences, but we can pardon.

It's also not reconciliation. This is the ideal, but we don't always have control over it. Reconciliation requires two people to agree. What if one of them won't or can't, as in the case of death?

It's not denying. Only when we acknowledge and come to terms with what was done to us can we truly forgive. Call it what it is. Open your heart. Be honest about it.

It's not forgetting. It is impossible to forget any significant event. We may choose NOT to remember.

Forgiveness is not an option. It is what we're called and empowered to do—releasing people with God's grace.

You might not be able to forget what someone did, but you can receive God's grace to go on...

> **"And which of you, having a servant plowing or tending sheep, will say to him when he has come in from the field, 'Come at once and sit down to eat'? But will he not rather say to him, 'Prepare something for my supper, and gird yourself and serve me till I have eaten and drunk, and afterward you will eat and drink'? Does he thank that servant because he did the things that were commanded him? I think not. So likewise you, when you have done all those things which you are commanded, say, 'We are unprofitable servants. We have done what was our duty to do' "** (Luke 17:7-10).

As I shared, my husband and I both came from broken homes. My parents divorced when I was three. My mother used to cry as she watched me stand by the window and wait for hours on end at the promise of my father's coming, and he wouldn't show up. This is very disappointing to a small child. I had family issues and instability all through my young life, which included alcohol and drug abuse in my father and stepfather. When my father died prematurely, it felt as if someone had pulled the rug out from under me. Many times going through the pain and trauma, a child will begin to expect disappointment.

If we put up walls to protect ourselves and keep others out, we go to defense mechanisms instead of trusting God to take care of it. We block out the love we need with the barriers we erect. Dennis used to hug people, but keep them at 'arm's length' in his heart. He reasoned, "I've been hurt before, so I will protect myself from being hurt again." How does that work? When you put walls up, then you even put walls up for God. We need to learn to let God restore our soul by experiencing His kind of unconditional agape love.

Some people have encountered situations of molestation or abandonment in childhood. We have expectations of others in these situations. Why didn't you help? Why didn't you do something?

As believers, sometimes we experience personal betrayal—even in Christian circles. One time, early in ministry, we had close missionary friends. We did everything we could to help them make the transition from the mission field. We all had a vision to do things together in ministry. God was leading us to start a church, but our friends had different expectations. As a result, they ended up severing their relationship with us. We had to learn to let go, forgive, and release them.

Another time, I had a huge chip on my shoulder and an antagonistic attitude toward my father-in-law. I felt as though he condescended to my husband and I really resented him for it, almost waiting for opportunities to have conflict with him. As a young believer, I remember reading about forgiveness, and I thought it would be impossible. When I began to understand that it was a choice, and that the Lord would empower me, I asked Him to help me see him the way that He did. Wow—if you're willing to yield to God's view and opinion, be ready for an adjustment. The next time I saw my father-in-law, I had a completely new kind of mercy and attitude toward him. I began relating to him differently and had a new compassion for him. Dennis was able to influence him and pray with him to receive God's love and salvation before he passed away.

Offenses can cause us to stumble. I cried out to God, "Lord, it was my best friend!" He answered, "I know what you mean." A father in the faith and life mentor, Dave Duell, told us at that difficult time, "When following God, you have to be willing to change friends." Not everyone is willing to travel the length with you or go where you are going. It's advisable to put up healthy boundaries in your life. If you lend someone money and they never pay you back, it's probably a good idea not to lend them any more money. You can say, "I love you, brother, but I'm probably not going to give you money this time."

It's not about us! Of course, we often take things so personally. But we need to reckon ourselves as dead and not be so offend-able. One of the greatest revelations that came out of this experience is that it wasn't *us* our friends were betraying. They had issues and would do the same to anyone in their path. Affliction and persecution come *for the Word's sake!* (see Mark 4:17) Remember, the enemy of our soul is after the Word germinating in our heart. That is a threat to the kingdom of darkness. But we choose, and Jesus won already. We can sabotage our own destiny by giving in to offenses or harboring betrayal. There are things going on in others' lives that have to be sorted through. We can't be so foolish to have unjust expectations of those not even capable of following through on their intentions. It takes time to build trust. We are all at different stages of development and growth. We all need to learn more about healthy boundaries (not walls).

Have you been hurt? Is the Holy Spirit tugging on your heart to forgive someone? Why not pray right now? Say, "Lord, I am opening up my heart to You. I forgive and release _____(name them). Having done so, I bless them and receive Your forgiveness for holding onto that offense. I expect healing and deliverance today. Thank You for freedom from this bondage!" We get to choose.

Betrayal is giving aid or information to an enemy or being false or disloyal in a cause. It's divulging a confidence or leading astray, deceiving.

When people let us down or disappoint us, no matter what the intention, if we respond to them as betrayal, it will dictate our actions. We'll find ourselves caught in a trap that could sabotage our destiny. Harboring a sense of betrayal feeds every aspect of unbelief and leads to certain failure. 'Harboring an offense' is like a boat in a marina, wintering there. That boat is anchored, and it's not going anywhere. Neither will we until we deal with our sense of betrayal! What are you allowing in your life that could lead you to betray Jesus or other people?

"Therefore, as *the* elect of God, holy and beloved, put on tender mercies, kindness, humility, meekness, longsuffering; bearing with one another, and forgiving one another, if anyone has a complaint against another; even as Christ forgave you, so you also

must do. **But above all these things put on love, which is the bond of perfection**" (Colossians 3:12-14).

All this is possible now because He lives inside of us.

Joseph

What are we allowing in our lives that could lead us to betray Jesus and/or others? Twenty-two years after betraying and selling him into slavery, Joseph's brothers stood before him (see Genesis 43-45). He was now Prime Minister over all of Egypt, the most powerful man on earth under Pharaoh himself. How would he deal with his brothers after all this time? What would we have done?

The integrity of Joseph's heart and character has impacted and challenged me. Why did Joseph make everyone leave the room except his brothers? He wanted to make sure that NO ONE would ever know what they had done! There was no one with him when he made himself known. We can choose the high road too, and not tell.

Even though Joseph held their very lives in his hands, he approached his brother in tears of compassion…

"Then Joseph could no longer control himself before all his attendants, and he cried out, 'Have everyone leave my presence!' So there was no one with Joseph when he made himself known to his brothers" (Genesis 45:1 NIV).

He didn't rub their noses in it, nor did he intimidate them…

"And he wept so loudly that the Egyptians heard him, and Pharaoh's household heard about it. Joseph said to his brothers, 'I am Joseph! Is my father still living?' But his brothers were not able to answer him, because they were terrified at his presence. Then Joseph said to his brothers, 'Come close to me.' When they had done so, he said, 'I am your brother Joseph, the one you sold into Egypt!'" (Genesis 45:2-4 NIV).

135

God has enough on each of us to bury us, but He won't tell. So why do we tell? Do we do it to punish?

"Perfect love drives out fear, because fear has to do with punishment" (1 John 4:18).

Do you like being punished? What if someone put you in a pit like Joseph, sold you on an auction block as a slave, sent you off to a strange man's house to be his servant, and then accused you of something you didn't do. Has anyone ever accused you of something you didn't do? Something rises up on the inside of you, and you need God's grace to see everything from His perspective!

"And now, do not be distressed and do not be angry with yourselves for selling me here, because it was to save lives that God sent me ahead of you" (Genesis 45:5 NIV).

Joseph held his brother's lives in his hands, but he did not intimidate them. He approached them with tears of compassion. Instead of exposing his brothers, Joseph covered their sins. He had a chance to be a victim, but chose to comfort them instead. He modeled something beautiful for us to behold in his place of security. We can choose not to put a manipulative guilt trip on someone.

Offenses happen every day, but we need to yield and submit to the grace of God every time an offense comes. You can take what was meant to destroy you, to get you off track, to keep you running around the mountain a few more years, and turn it around by blessing others.

We can't do this in our own self-effort and strength—we need the grace of God! Our forgiveness is worthless unless we make it possible for others to forgive themselves as Joseph did for his brothers. This is one of the most empowering stories in Scripture. This kind of response from the heart will set you up to live out your dreams!

Forgiving yourself is so important too. In order not to be in bondage in our own hearts, we need to forgive and release ourselves, realizing that Jesus' sacrifice was for us. He emptied Himself—Jesus as a Man, full of the Holy Spirit. Self-forgiveness had to be Paul's hurdle too...

"For you have heard of my former conduct in Judaism, how I persecuted the church of God beyond measure and *tried to* destroy it" (Galatians 1:13).

Forgiving yourself is a tough thing. We need to release ourselves for the things we've done. Jesus became sin for us (see 2 Corinthians 5:21).

Paul also preached grace as no one else, and this led many to slander him and his teaching by accusing him of encouraging people to sin. He was misquoted, misunderstood, and misrepresented. This same thing happens to many leaders in ministry today. Although I have never yet been beaten or imprisoned, I have felt this way multiple times, and I'm trusting God for the final outcome.

Our beloved mentor, Dr. Jim Richards, always says, "The TRUTH that has the most potential to set you free also has the most potential to offend you. The TRUTH you need to set you free is the TRUTH you don't believe."

You are BORN TO BE WILD! Conception is easy, but it's the pains of pregnancy and delivery that inconvenience us. There are no abortions in God's plan! Let's bring His life forth without sabotaging it by taking *offense* and *betrayals*. Let's live out the destiny of the blueprint of our Daddy's design for us. Let the rivers flow!

Chapter 13
Garden Party

The Garden of Eden was a picturesque place described as pleasant to see. A river even went out of Eden to water the garden. God rested on the seventh day, saying His work was finished. Since God never sleeps nor slumbers, we know He wasn't tired (see Psalm 121:4). He rested because creation was complete. The garden was perfect—a good place for a garden party. God wants us to experience this restored kingdom living which was His intention from the beginning. This is for the rest of your life!

Man's only job was to guard the garden, but after the Fall...

"Therefore the LORD God sent him out of the garden of Eden to till the ground from which he was taken" (Genesis 3:23).

Our works began! That was a big lifestyle change for sure. So this brings us to a thorough look at restoration in all its forms and facets. The whole plan of redemption is God's buy-back. The outworking of it is in our relationship with Jesus. Are we guarding the finished work of Christ?

"But those things which God foretold by the mouth of all His prophets, that the Christ would suffer, He has thus fulfilled. Repent therefore and be converted, that your sins may be blotted out, so that times of refreshing may come from the presence of the Lord, and that He may send Jesus Christ, who was preached to you before, whom heaven must receive until the times of restoration of all things, which God has spoken by the mouth of all His holy prophets since the world began" (Acts 3:18-21).

Being in ministry for more than 25 years, I've seen people come and go. I've seen them high and low. I have purposed to release my personal expectations and judgments that would bog me down. I see God's image in people and choose to believe the best. I know the devotion and sacrifices people make for their families and in the kingdom of God. I also know betrayal all too well. My greatest desire after all these things is to see restoration take place in the heart, mind, and soul of people that are hurting.

As in the book of Acts, the local church (a living organism) is the place of practical administration in the body of Christ. In the Old Testament, how the priests carried out their duties can speak to us of how tasks are fulfilled, accomplished, and achieved. In a sense, it's an assignment. In the Old Testament, the Levites were given directives on how to carry out the procedures of their duties. In Numbers 4:20-25, the Hebrew word rendered 'performing the service' could also be translated 'war the warfare.' Using your God-given gifts in His service is warfare!

"From whom the whole body, joined and knit together by what every joint supplies, according to the effective working by which every part does its share, causes growth of the body for the edifying of itself in love" (Ephesians 4:16, emphasis mine).

We've become tangled up in just how this is worked out in our lives. Too often too few carry the biggest load while the majority of the others are spectators. Your service to God is a gift, its acting on what you believe and it is warfare!

> "From thirty years old and above, even to fifty years old, you shall number them, all who enter to perform the service, to do the work in the tabernacle of meeting. This *is* the service of the families of the Gershonites, in serving and carrying: They shall carry the curtains of the tabernacle and the tabernacle of meeting *with* its covering, the covering of badger skins that *is* on it, the screen for the door of the tabernacle of meeting"' (Numbers 4:23-25).

These were the detailed particulars that were performed by the priests and musicians. How did these thirty to fifty year olds do it? By fulfilling their role. They each contributed their service by fulfilling a task.

We each have a purpose and a destiny! Remember, in the Old Testament the work was never finished. As a New Testament saint, our part is to flow with our grace gift by believing what was done for us. But rather than striving to achieve, in our New Covenant we can adopt an attitude of believing, coming boldly before His throne of grace with this posture...

> "And every priest stands ministering daily and offering repeatedly the same sacrifices, which can never take away sins. But this Man, after He had offered one sacrifice for sins forever, sat down at the right hand of God, from that time waiting till His enemies are made His footstool" (Hebrews 10:11-13).

Think of the perfection of the Garden of Eden and how God rested on the seventh day. The prophets foretold by God the sending of Jesus. Now in this time of restoration and refreshing from the presence of the Lord, are we guarding the already finished work or are we tilling the ground in this garden (that is work and self-effort)? If we are guarding an already finished work, we'll probably have a garden party!

> "There remains therefore a rest for the people of God" (Hebrews 4:9).

There's a place where you cease from your own labors, and you must labor to enter into this place, which is rest...

"For he who has entered His rest has himself also ceased from his works as God *did* from His. Let us therefore be diligent to enter that rest" (Hebrews 4:10-11).

There is no more combating a defeated foe. Instead, it's an enforcement of his defeat. Our work is 'believing'. The warfare has ended in the finished work of Christ. Now the work is finished. There remains believing the truth. We are seated with Christ. Our enemies are our footstool. Will we maintain our 'throne attitude' where we have come for help in time of need? Recognize that the enemy is under our feet! Ask yourself, "Am I fighting *for* victory or *from* victory?

To Will & To Do

"For it is God who works in you both to will and to do for His good pleasure" (Philippians 2:13).

God is always leading our born-again spirit, under the influence of the Holy Spirit, in the direction of His will. That's what pleases Him. Yet, we have a say in what takes place in our lives. God puts it in, but we have to work it out!

Verse 13 reveals God's divine enablement that wills and is able to perform His bidding in our lives. But there is an effort on our part too. We have to work it out. This work needs to be understood in the light of the labor spoken of in Hebrews 4. We are to cease from trust in ourselves and rest in the Lord. That takes effort!

"Work out (cultivate, carry out to the goal, and fully complete) your own salvation with reverence *and* awe and trembling (self-distrust, with serious caution, tenderness of conscience, watchfulness against temptation, timidly shrinking from whatever might offend God and discredit the name of Christ)" (Philippians 2:13 AMPC).

Sounds like we're planning a party! I love the whole event-planning opportunity—from assessing the budget, to choosing the caterers, to arranging the flowers, décor, and music. It's an intentional event with celebration in mind and party guests coming over to celebrate together.

Throw Yourself a Garden Party

Just what are we celebrating? Well, there's a reckoning for the seasons of our lives and the storms we've come through with damage and loss. There's a turnaround through trusting God! I want to thank Him before I see it come to pass.

"My brethren, count it all joy when you fall into various trials" (James 1:2).

Our beloved mentor, Dave Duell, often quoted this verse using another paraphrase translation to declare that it read, "Throw yourself a party!"

"Knowing that the testing of your faith produces patience. But let patience have *its* perfect work, that you may be perfect and complete, lacking nothing" (James 1:3-4).

Notice that it's 'working' patience, like exercising a muscle. Patience is a form of faith over time. It's a verb, not a passive response. It's believing, which is active, and can be described as a calm endurance with some longevity in trusting in God, Whom you know is good.

The only thing left to do in a garden that's finished is to sow seeds! It's our position now as people at the garden party to enjoy the festivities. God's restoring us to our original design in relationship with Him and His finished work. The work has been done. Now we are living the life, just sowing the seeds, planting the Word, sharing the gospel, and telling the story. It's a garden party!

Any thought, idea, mindset, doctrine, or fear that would refute what the Bible tells us about the victorious death, burial, and resurrection of Jesus, and how we share in it, is a stronghold. We can simply make it a way of life to spend time in

142

reflective, meditative thought on a regular basis. In a physically relaxed state, our brainwaves slow down, making our intellectual mind less dominant. It's in this state of peace that we start recognizing the still, small voice of God.

Lost & Found

The story of the Prodigal Son paints such a clear picture of God's heart and attitude of celebration. It's one in a series of three stories in the book of Luke where Jesus revealed God's heart of restoration towards something He lost (see Luke 15 for the stories of the Lost Sheep, Lost Coin, and Lost Son). Our good friend and bible teacher, Ed Elliott, tells the story so well...

"What do you think would have happened to the Prodigal Son if he had run into his elder brother before he got to experience the love, acceptance, embrace, and kiss of his father? I think he may have never made it home. His elder brother's view of their father was radically different from who the father really was. I believe the elder brother would have scolded and condemned his younger brother for being selfish, thoughtless, reckless, and living a sin-filled life. He would have probably made the Prodigal think that his father was so angry with him he never wanted to see him again. At that point of hopelessness, the Prodigal would have changed his course. How we portray God to the people we meet on a daily basis will determine the path they take in life. My desire is for people to experience our heavenly Father's unconditional love and forgiveness as a reality in their hearts. We never know when we act as God's embrace and kiss someone searching for the kind of love only God can provide"

My favorite part is the father's response to his older (religious) son...

"'Son, you are always with me, and all that I have is yours. It was right that we should make merry and be glad, for your brother was dead and is alive again, and was lost and is found'" (Luke 15:31-32).

In essence, "You could have had a party anytime!" Let's celebrate the finished work of Jesus and have a garden party!

143

Chapter 14

Restore

There is power and promise in restoration. And there are many different facets to restoration...

> **"Brethren, if a man is overtaken in any trespass, you who *are* spiritual restore such a one in a spirit of gentleness, considering yourself lest you also be tempted"** (Galatians 6:1).

On the Mend

The word '**overtaken**' carries the idea of something that comes upon a person by surprise. Also, the word translated as '**trespass**' means a side-slip, unintentional error, or willful transgression (see Andrew Wommack's Living Commentary). Paul was giving these instructions about how to help someone who is sincere, but in error. The spiritual ones, whom the apostle instructs to restore those who are overtaken in a fault, are those who are dependent upon and led by the Holy Spirit. That's how we can humanly restore one another.

The word translated '**restore**' means to set a bone that has been broken. It takes time for broken bones to mend, and usually activities have to be restricted during the healing process. Likewise, spiritual restoration takes time and usually necessitates a change of routine. If the individual goes back to the same circumstances, chances are they will make the same wrong choices as before. Also, just as setting a broken bone in the natural is painful but necessary, the restoration process is always painful.

Failing to deal with issues completely because it is painful is similar to not setting a broken bone. The bone will never be straight again. That's such a prophetic picture of what happens to us in life if we don't get restored. We can become permanently twisted.

"The crooked heart will not prosper; the lying tongue tumbles into trouble" (Proverbs 17:20 NLT).

Enduring a moment of pain as the bone is set will let the bone then mend properly and become as strong as it was before. Just as a cast protects the broken bone from further injury, a person who has fallen should be surrounded by brothers and sisters who are committed to keeping the fallen individual from making the injury worse. Submission to loving spiritual authority is just as important to a person who has fallen as a cast is to someone with a broken bone. Until the healing is complete, the cast and the curtailed lifestyle have to be maintained even though it may be inconvenient and uncomfortable. Trying to return to "normal" prematurely can prevent the bone from ever being completely healed. This is a natural truth regarding restoration. It's a foundational concept for us to grasp. We can be stronger than before!

True Restoration

But let's also consider another form of restoration…

"*People* do not despise a thief if he steals to satisfy himself when he is starving. Yet *when* he is found, he must restore sevenfold; he may have to give up all the substance of his house" (Proverbs 6:31).

When a thief is caught, they have to restore! Even throughout the Old Testament we see a picture painted for us…

"In all cases of illegal possession of an ox, a donkey, a sheep, a garment, or any other lost property about which somebody says, 'This is mine,' both parties are to bring their cases before the judges. The one whom the judges declare guilty must pay back double to the other" (Exodus 22:9 NIV).

There is here a clarity of understanding the Scripture, a restitution between parties. This depicts the one who opposed us being made to release what was taken from us, or give restitution for what was lost. How much more would this be in the spirit realm, and in our reality lived out on the earth? There is significant biblical precedent for restoration! I pray that you will take hold of this.

"If a man steals an ox or a sheep, and slaughters it or sells it, he shall restore five oxen for an ox and four sheep for a sheep" (Exodus 22:1).

Can you see the precedent for even more? One stolen, four or five restored. We can gain from it. If we suffer a loss, there can be a greater restoration!

Restoring the Years

On one of the saddest days of my life, when my Mother passed away, I found a photo with the words below written in her very handwriting…

"I will restore to you the years that the swarming locust has eaten, the crawling locust, the consuming locust, and the chewing locust" (Joel 2:25).

It was a Polaroid picture of my Mom with my stepfather, who had spent a month at a treatment center. It was an alcohol rehab that he had checked into decades before as they had teetered on the verge of divorce. She had believed a promise from God's Word in the book of Joel, and he had experienced salvation in his life and a complete deliverance from alcohol addiction.

He came to know the Lord there through a radical conversion experience while going through the twelve-step program. Before that, he had only known childhood religion, which had left him disillusioned. But as he humbled himself in that state of desperation—he encountered the goodness and love of God. That began a miraculous turnaround for our whole family.

As I looked at that picture, the Lord challenged me at that very moment, on that very day, to trust Him to restore even this premature home-going of my Mom. I knew I wouldn't have my Mother back, but if I could give Him the circumstance—this loss—He would turn it around.

God's heart longs to restore to you whatever the locust—a picture of the enemy—has eaten, especially your lost time. If you've been living in regret over years lost to bondage and addiction, depression, or a bottoming out in your life goals, God can restore and redeem. You see, He lives outside of time and can supernaturally restore to you all the wasted time you have spent in fear, worry, doubt, guilt, condemnation, sickness, and bondage. Whether you have lost precious time, a loved one, broken relationships, or if you've been robbed through sickness or disease—trust God to recover your life. Don't give up, and don't give in!

According to the Brown Briggs Lexicon, the Greek word for restoration means "The restoration not only of true theocracy but also of that more perfect state of even physical things which existed before the fall." I love it! God is working out a restoration for all mankind. Jesus is the Door. We need to be good

147

receivers of what He has for us when we open up and let Him in. God is so good at turning things around!

> "I will exalt you, LORD, for you lifted me out of the depths and did not let my enemies gloat over me. LORD my God, I called to you for help, and you healed me. You, LORD, brought me up from the realm of the dead; you spared me from going down to the pit...weeping may stay for the night, but rejoicing comes in the morning...You turned my wailing into dancing; you removed my sackcloth and clothed me with joy, that my heart may sing your praises and not be silent. LORD my God, I will praise you forever" (Psalm 30:1-3, 5, 11-12 NIV).

I am just now grasping the full awareness—just now in my fifties—that God is a Restorer! I have chosen to relinquish all the brokenness, disappointment, hurt, betrayal, and loss that I have experienced in life into the hands of the One Who loves me the very most. By faith, I believe His promises to restore. I may not know how or when, but I know He is faithful to take it and restore it completely.

Before the fall of man, there was no disease, lack, depression, divorce, wars, strife, or death. Everything lost—including years and time—God can redeem if we believe and expect that He will. And part of restoration is rest...

> "The LORD *is* my shepherd; I shall not want. He makes me to lie down in green pastures; He leads me beside the still waters. He restores my soul; He leads me in the paths of righteousness for His name's sake" (Psalm 23:1-3).

Will we open up our mind, will, and emotions, and begin to allow the recovery work to take place within?

Restoration of Past Times & Lost Relationships

When Dennis and I began in ministry in the early 1990s with launching our local church, simultaneously our close friends were going into mission work. As a passionate, adventurous couple, Chris & Terri were launching off to Europe with a plan to learn the language and preach the good news gospel to those who had become stoic, intellectual, and humanistic in a culture that was once Christian. We hosted a going away celebration reception for them as they left for the mission field of France. We supported them with our prayers and our whole new church family did also with monthly giving. We took periodic mission trips with teams of people over to assist them in their new endeavors and in fulfilling their vision. We enjoyed a close bond of friendship, and experienced great exploits and precious times together in different places in the world while in ministry at the same time. Where they were in southern France proved to be a very challenging mission field even though it had such romantic and tourist appeal. The last day of our tour there, our dear friend became very sick.

The news of Chris getting sick shocked and saddened us, especially after finding out the blood tests showed he was battling leukemia. We all stood together in believing God's promises and saw positive progress at several turns with his health. We watched the difficulty of being so far away from friends and family. After four years of walking by faith—struggling with fears, having extensive medical procedures, continuing in the church and mission work, trusting God for healing, moving back to the United States with his family, and then going into the hospital—Chris gave up the fight. Even though it was a loss of a battle, he won the war by entering into his eternal home with Jesus.

We all shared in the sorrow, disappointment, loss, and grief, but allowed the Lord to turn it around. Now, we know we don't get that beloved friend back on this earth, but because of the promise of God we knew He would bring about a restoration. It really takes a perceptive heart that is open and expectant for that to come to pass. In the case of our dear friend, Terri, we have seen a living testimony walked out over the course of ten years. God has brought His promises to manifestation with her newest husband, Dennis, who is also experiencing the faithful restoration of a loss of a relationship through death. These two are in love and functioning as a team working together serving God and seeing His kingdom advance. God's abundant, life-giving restoration has been exemplified through Terri's life right before our very eyes!

"Instead of your shame *you shall have* double *honor,* and *instead of* confusion they shall rejoice in their portion. Therefore in their land they shall possess double; everlasting joy shall be theirs" (Isaiah 61:7).

Ruth

My good friend Terri's story has been so very similar to the Bible story of Ruth. She was young, married for a few years, and looking ahead to a fruitful family life. Then, in Ruth's story, her husband suddenly died. Overnight, all her hopes crashed; her future, uncertain. Although her mother-in-law urged her to return to her own town to start over, the young woman refused. Clinging to her mother-in-law, she declared:

"Wherever you go, I will go; and wherever you lodge, I will lodge; your people *shall be* my people, and your God, my God" (Ruth 1:16).

One of the most beautiful love stories in the Bible—the story of Ruth—unfolds. Beyond being just a love story, and a picture of our redemption in Christ, it's also a clear portrait of God's amazing restoration. When Ruth followed Naomi (her mother-in-law) to Israel, she soon found herself in a less-than-ideal position. With no husband to protect her, she was a Moabitess living among a people often in conflict with Moab. In the natural, it seemed as if the odds were stacked against her.

150

But Ruth didn't brood on her negative situation. Her declaration of faith in the God of Israel revealed her heartfelt dependence on the Lord, Whom she looked to for favor and divine opportunities. We can learn from her response of trusting the Lord…

> **"So Ruth the Moabitess said to Naomi, 'Please let me go to the field, and glean heads of grain after *him* in whose sight I may find favor.' And she said to her, 'Go, my daughter'"** (Ruth 2:2).

As she sought employment and support for her mother-in-law and herself, Ruth's faith in God became her launching pad to God's incredible restoration in her life. First, God gave her favor to glean the barley harvest in the field of Boaz, a wealthy man who happened to be a close relative of her late husband. Being extremely kind to Ruth, Boaz allowed her to gather more than enough grain in his field for both her and her mother-in-law's daily needs.

But God had so much more in mind than merely *getting by* for Ruth. He blessed her with a husband—Boaz himself—and with a child, Obed, who became the grandfather of King David and whose name shows up in the ancestry of Jesus Christ. Ruth herself is named in His genealogy as well (see Matthew 1:5-6; Luke 3:32). When it seemed impossible in the natural, Ruth's life went from tragedy to triumph. Imagine going from having no family to having a loving husband and son, from being destitute to being well-provided for. She went from being an outsider to being not just an accepted and well-loved member of society, but part of the lineage of the Messiah Himself. What a turnaround! What amazing restoration!

I know because of being alongside of my close friend, prayer partner, and co-laborer in ministry—whom I experienced much of this pain and emotional loss with her. I understood her hopes being crushed, and walked with her through an even more negative series of events that I couldn't even begin to cover here. I understand how the deaths of many beloved relatives and friends can shatter dreams and leave us with a bleak future.

151

Is that you today? Maybe you're even saying to yourself, "It's over for me!" I know from the promises of God's Word, from experiences with the Lord myself, and through my good friend Terri that God desires for us to test Him and trust Him at His very Word. Don't give in to believing the lies of the enemy that aim to sink you into depression and hopelessness.

Let the restoration begin! No man can do this but the Lord. He lives outside of time, and can supernaturally restore to you all the wasted time you have spent in fear, worry, doubt, guilt, condemnation, sickness, and bondage. Whether you have lost valuable time, broken relationships, or been afflicted with disease that has robbed you of your health or your youth, let His Word strengthen your heart and life today. Jesus is…

"**Called Repairer of Broken Walls, Restorer of Streets with Dwellings**" (Isaiah 58:12).

Christ came, finished His work, and commissioned us to become repairers of broken walls and restorers of streets with dwellings. Jesus promised…

"**He who believes in Me, the works that I do he will do also; and greater *works* than these he will do, because I go to My Father**" (John 14:12).

We are here to repair and restore in His name!

God Is Our Healer

God promises:

"**'For I will restore health to you and heal you of your wounds,' says the Lord, 'Because they called you an outcast *saying:* 'This *is* Zion; no one seeks her'**" (Jeremiah 30:17).

Think of people you may know who are bankrupt emotionally or physically. Such a desolate inheritance reveals a promise that was never claimed, assigned, or accessed. Promises of well-being, fruitfulness, and peace belong to people—and even to whole nations. When you meet someone clearly missing their life assignment because of a destructive cycle, ask the Lord to reveal the desolate inheritance that is awaiting fulfillment. That person may be called to leadership in ministry but is using their gifts in ways that are more culturally familiar. That individual, that leader is...

"God's handiwork, created in Christ Jesus to do good works, which God prepared in advance for us to do" (Ephesians 2:10 NIV).

The promise has not expired. Today is the day of salvation!

No One Says "Restore!"

"But this *is* a people robbed and plundered; all of them are snared in holes, and they are hidden in prison houses; they are for prey, and no one delivers; for plunder, and no one says, 'Restore!'" (Isaiah 42:22).

Who really believes that God will bring about a restoration from our loss or pain? So many believers have been confused, not understanding that God is NOT the source of their pain, loss, or problems; so they're surprised to realize that God wants to restore. After reading this Old Testament passage, I asked the Lord myself, "Why didn't the people say 'restore'?" Speaking directly to my heart, He answered and said, "Because no one believes that I will."

The Hebrew phrase 'tikkun olam' means world repair. The phrase originated in classic rabbinic literature and was recited three times daily by Jews in prayer. The idea of repairing the world is God's idea, and He calls us to be involved.

God can use anyone. Whatever has been broken due to the fall of man, God will repair and restore—and He will use you in the process. Don't rely too heavily on your areas of expertise. God is not looking for experts. He's looking for people who are willing to follow His direction and trust Him.

Repair and restoration don't spring from anxiety—they flow from hope. People who see the unseen bring heaven to earth. Change brings discomfort. Are you still waiting for a breakthrough that seems out of reach? Is it really? How might your perceptions be misleading you? Ask God what His plans ahead look like for you. How does He want to use you to turn skeptics into kingdom believers and spectators into His kingdom family on the go? This is a new season of opportunity. The Lord is going before us right now and making the path straight for us. Obstacles and things that have opposed you are going to be removed!

Financial Restoration

"I will give you hidden treasures, riches stored in secret places, so that you may know that I am the Lord, the God of Israel, who summons you by name. For the sake of Jacob my servant, of Israel my chosen, I summon you by name and bestow on you a title of honor" (Isaiah 45:3-4 NIV).

God is releasing plans and strategies to get you repaid for your losses and to help prepare you for what is coming. I see strategies, accelerated blessing and favor flowing from heaven. A major part of receiving this is to position yourself for the new and not give up nor believe the lies that you have failed or will not make it!

"**Fight the good fight of faith**" (1 Timothy 6:12).

There is just one battle we are called to fight in our New Covenant, and it's the good fight of faith. When we position ourselves—our thoughts, feelings, and beliefs—with the finished work of Jesus, we are resisting the devil. We don't want to become devil-conscious instead of Christ-conscious and Christ-centered. That's just the carnal mind, which is in opposition to God and won't experience the law of the Spirit of life in Christ Jesus. New Testament warfare Scriptures identify our battleground as the soul—our mind, will, and emotions. The struggle centers there in the realm of our thoughts and feelings. As we focus upon our "in Him" awareness, then we'll stay in peace.

Personally, I'm in a place of rest and believing for a restoration of many things in my life. God's promises are mine in Christ, and I know He's a good God. My heart is expectant and I'm smiling at the future. This is for you too. Thank God.

Chapter 15
Home

God—He's at home in heaven and in your heart (if received). We share that value and truth. My recollections of home life were of a very warm childhood with caring, loving grandparents and a single mother raising us together. When your parents divorced even before you have memories, you don't know what you're missing until much later. In my home in Old East St. Louis, we had backyard barbeques on Sunday afternoons with visiting cousins and family-like next-door neighbors all interacting with the children playing on swing sets. There were open cornfields where we flew kites on windy days—all treasured memories. But I especially remember the security I felt even with divorce and dysfunction in our circumstances. My Grandmother made it all so safe by directing so much of her time and attention our way while rocking us in a rocking chair and singing songs aloud that I can still sing today. Grandma listened to us—and answered—our unending random questions.

I remember my little sister jabbering as we occupied ourselves with cushion and blanket makeshift toys. My mother lived there too, but had to work so much, she made 'appearances' like a celebrity. Sometimes my Dad would stop in to see us. And Grandpa was the life of the party (both of them had a drinking problem). In his fun-natured ways, he brought home candy suckers for all the girls (sisters and cousins) on his weekly payday. As zany and unplanned as our life drama may have been, in hindsight I can see that my grandparents did what they could (or what they knew) to make it a memorable and meaningful bond of love for us in our home. They cared, invested, and were our example. Thank God my Mom had the skill and diligence to work, and to make a way and a living for us.

Escape Traps

Have you heard the funny saying, "Save the drama for your Mama"? Every home and family has some drama. And I'm sure there are varied degrees of extremes in the toxicity in relationships and conflict within families. One of the most practical things I've learned as an adult coming through relational issues in my own family and helping other people has to do with setting healthy boundaries with family and friends, and living out forgiveness. I am not referring to building walls for self-protection against others. We really do need other people; God created us that way. True spirituality can be measured by our ability to get along with others.

You can't get to where you're going if you're easily ensnared in everybody else's business! I'm just saying it like it is. People even tried to do that to Jesus, that is draw Him into their family drama...

"Then one from the crowd said to Him, 'Teacher, tell my brother to divide the inheritance with me.' But He said to him, 'Man, who made Me a judge or an arbitrator over you?'" (Luke 12:13-14).

We can't get involved in a brothers' fight about money. Everyone wanted the Lord to take their side. They wanted Jesus to say who was right and who was wrong—they wanted Him for their own purposes. So how does one handle a situation like that? Simple! Give them the truth to work with, and let them all make their own choices and decisions. If they have no regard for truth, then we cannot help them. That's how we get into codependent traps—trying to help such people. It's just one classic example how we get our lives in trouble, all entangled in strife and misunderstanding. Sometimes the complexities of all that can detour our lives for decades!

Knowing our righteousness in Christ and our identity in Him enables us to be confident and secure in His love…

"If it is possible, as much as depends on you, live peaceably with all men" (Romans 12:18).

This verse advocates living peaceably with all people, yet the very wording reveals that this isn't always possible. We are not responsible for other people's actions. We must pursue peace, even when we're not at fault, but the other individuals do have a choice. We should be sure that we are at peace with all people—whether or not they are at peace with us is their decision (see Life for Today Commentary by Andrew Wommack).

We can live in peace and get our values from the One Who gave His life for us, instead of all the chaotic directions that we get pulled in. Remember when Jesus could do no mighty works in His own hometown because of their unbelief? (see Matthew 13:58) We can give guidance and support through the Word of God, but we must have enough healthy boundaries in place so as not to get snared into others' issues and blamed for their problems and destructive choices. Even the sinless, Son of God would not get in the middle of their mess. Of course He cares, and He gives us the truth to help us make our own decisions based on His Spirit's wisdom in every situation. We all want to prioritize our circle of influence. We all desire restoration in our families and homes that only God can give. To see this, we must increase the capacity of our heart to receive the goodness of God in our lives. It starts on the inside first—with how we see Him and see ourselves!

"What you do with your grace is up to you!" (Charis Bible College Instructor Barry Bennett) Remember, it's His enablement, empowerment, and divine ability to do what you could not do. Embrace the uncertainty that some of the best chapters of your life won't have a title until much later. It's all unfolding, a continuing journey of—not an arrival, but—living in the now.

Hometown Boy

Remember Jesus in His childhood—as a twelve-year-old boy? His priorities showed up early in life, and were clearly connected to knowing His identity. He would have been considered a good 'hometown boy.'

> **"His parents went to Jerusalem every year at the Feast of the Passover. And when He was twelve years old, they went up to Jerusalem according to the custom of the feast. When they had finished the days, as they returned, the Boy Jesus lingered behind in Jerusalem. And Joseph and His mother did not know *it;* but supposing Him to have been in the company, they went a day's journey, and sought Him among *their* relatives and acquaintances. So when they did not find Him, they returned to Jerusalem, seeking Him. Now so it was *that* after three days they found Him in the temple, sitting in the midst of the teachers, both listening to them and asking them questions. And all who heard Him were astonished at His understanding and answers. So when they saw Him, they were amazed; and His mother said to Him, "Son, why have You done this to us? Look, Your father and I have sought You anxiously." And He said to them, "Why did you seek Me? Did you not know that I must be about My Father's business?"** (Luke 2:41-49).

After marrying my husband Dennis, we raised our family together in three homes, especially the house we built and remodeled over the course of thirty years. That same one we sold to buy and enjoy a beach house on the East Coast. We have homes in different places. And we've been transitioning, with our congregation, from the facility that has served as our church home for over twenty years. However, we know in our hearts that our true home is in heaven. We're citizens there for eternity! But while we're still here on earth, we must live with an eternal perspective. My story, and yours, continues to be written as we live Acts 29 (right now) in preparation for arrival in our true home.

After God's Own Heart

The Word describes King David as a...
 "**Man after His own heart**" (1 Samuel 13:14).
This was confirmed in the New Testament, as God said...
 "**I have found David the *son* of Jesse, a man after My *own* heart**" (Acts 13:22).
Why? Because he desired the same priority that God wanted! David was more than one who was just 'quick to repent' or change his mind. God is after your heart, and He wants your heart to be after Him. He wants you rooted and established in the truth of His Word—not just in your head, but in your heart!
 "**Do not be carried about with various and strange doctrines. For *it is* good that the heart be established by grace**" (Hebrews 13:9).

God's Resting Place

The Psalms of King David are full of prophetic, messianic, and historical insights...
 "**LORD, remember David *and* all his afflictions; how he swore to the LORD, *and* vowed to the Mighty One of Jacob: 'Surely I will**

159

not go into the chamber of my house, or go up to the comfort of my bed; I will not give sleep to my eyes *or* slumber to my eyelids, until I find a place for the LORD, a dwelling place for the Mighty One of Jacob.' Behold, we heard of it in Ephrathah; we found it in the fields of the woods. Let us go into His tabernacle; let us worship at His footstool. Arise, O LORD, to Your resting place, You and the ark of Your strength" (Psalm 132:1-8).

David determined to quickly find a place to build a temple to the Lord. This passage of Scripture stresses his intense desire to honor God by building Him a temple. The tabernacle of Moses and, later, the temple of Solomon were of great significance and importance to these Old Testament saints. But the simple truth today is: We are the temple of the Lord (see 1 Corinthians 6:19). It's not the place where we meet today that is important. I shared earlier how we have sold the facility in which our local church met. We may rent a very adequate space to gather, celebrate, and expand in size as well as continue meeting house to house to reach out and disciple others through multiplying home groups and the ministry that flows from each believer.

The Ark of the Covenant

David understood what the Ark of the Covenant represented. The Ark of the Covenant had 'rested' in Kirjath Jearim for twenty years (see 1 Samuel 7:1-2) where there's no mention of blessing before David began bringing it to Jerusalem (see 2 Samuel 6:1-11). God's blessing came upon the house of Obed-Edom—because of the ark—while hosting the ark for only three months (see 2 Samuel 6:11-12). Then David made a seven mile journey to bring the ark back to Jerusalem. He had a great revelation of the value of the ark. He was a man on a mission!

"Then David danced before the Lord with all *his* might; and David *was* wearing a linen ephod" (this was a priestly garment, not a kingly one; 2 Samuel 6:14).

In his humility and passion for the Lord, he wore priestly garments, not his kingly ones, as he worshiped. David remembered where he came from. This passage goes on to share how Saul's daughter, Michal (David's wife), despised him in her heart (2 Samuel 6:16). She remained barren her whole life (2 Samuel 6:20, 23). A bitter and envious attitude caused her to be unfruitful.

Parallel this with the Pharisee's reaction to Jesus entering Jerusalem on a donkey during Passover right before His crucifixion. The religious leaders of the day became indignant when they heard the children crying out in the temple...

"Hosanna to the Son of David!" (Matthew 21:15).

Just like Michal remained barren for the rest of her life for mocking David for worshiping, so these religious leaders were completely fruitless and unproductive in God's eyes. This is serious business! Each one of us needs to deal with our own heart for despising worshipers' hearts and actions. Remember the ark 'housed' the presence of God.

"And so it was, when those bearing the ark of the LORD had gone six paces, that he sacrificed oxen and fatted sheep" (2 Samuel 6:13).

Why would David make a burnt offering sacrifice every six paces? This pictures how by the blood of Jesus we are cleansed, and made righteous and holy. David was continually conscious of our righteousness in it. What insight he had of the value of the ark, and how he desired to get it **home** to Jerusalem.

"Then King David rose to his feet and said, 'Hear me, my brethren and my people: I _had_ it in my heart to build a house of rest for the ark of the covenant of the LORD, and for the footstool of our God, and had made preparations to build it" (1 Chronicles 28:2, emphasis mine).

Isn't a footstool something a person puts their feet on at home? This identifies the tabernacle of the Lord as His footstool, or the place where He

161

dwelled. In Isaiah 66:1, the Lord spoke through the prophet that the earth was his footstool. So—get this picture—He's at home in the whole earth. In traveling so much for the last 25 years, I've learned to be at home in the whole earth. God is flowing through us to the people He loves everywhere!

If you could see God in heaven as He truly is, you'd lay aside this derogatory picture of an old judge looming and leaning over the edge, ready to strike us down with lightning bolts from the heavens. Instead, the true picture is God sitting on His throne, kicked-back with His feet up on a footstool. What a snapshot of rest!

There are so many Old Testament types and shadows that reveal a picture of God's rest for our lives. Now, don't mistake this for your passivity or inactivity—quite the contrary. It's still godly to be diligent, and faith expresses itself in Holy Spirit directed and inspired activity (see James 1:22-25; Titus 3:8, 14). But it's all about what we believe and who we believe in on a heart level.

I pray you have a colorful picture of energized and empowered fulfillment of purpose and destiny rising within you. This will unfold in a supernatural way as you believe in a good God Who accomplished the work. He already sees the end from the beginning (see Isaiah 46:10). See yourself in the fulfillment of these prophetic passages. Live alert, aware, connected, attentive, and filled with faith. God's grace will enable you to walk it out. This is our time to accomplish more than ever before with God's miraculous ability demonstrated on our behalf. This is our time to be light in gross darkness—let's shine bright! (see Philippians 2:12-16)

Meet & Speak

In Psalm 132, David didn't say, "God, give me a place where I can sleep." No, he vowed not to sleep until he had determined a place to build the temple to the Lord (see verses 2-5). Stay with me here...

The Ark of the Covenant or the throne of the Lord typifies God's presence. God's presence dwelled in the ark. Isn't it interesting that David is the one who concerned himself with transporting the ark? David made God's objective his objective. The Ark of the Covenant is all about Jesus—His presence and His finished work! This is what we can rest in—what He accomplished for us.

What was inside the Ark? It contained a gold pot of manna, Aaron's budding rod, and the Ten Commandments. All these represent man's rebellion against God's provision, authority, and law. Guess what? They're all in a box with a lid on it—covered by the mercy seat with the blood from the sacrifice on it. What a poignant picture for us today. Don't open it! Don't look at your sin! We have been cleansed by the blood of Jesus once and for all!

> **"And the cherubim shall stretch out _their_ wings above, covering the mercy seat with their wings, and they shall face one another; the faces of the cherubim _shall be_ toward the mercy seat. You shall put <u>the mercy seat on top of the ark</u>, and in the <u>ark you shall put the Testimony that I will give you</u>. And there I will meet with you, and I will speak with you from above the mercy seat, from between the two cherubim which _are_ on the ark of the Testimony, about everything which I will give you in commandment to the children of Israel"** (Exodus 25:20-22, emphasis mine).

God purposely expressed that He put the testimony (the Ten Commandments) inside, underneath the mercy seat, which is positioned HIGHER than the Ten Commandments (verse 21). Notice verse 22...

> **"And there I will meet with you, and I will speak with you from above the mercy seat."**

Note the significance of the placement of the mercy seat above. God's priority is to meet with us and speak with us! His mercy triumphs over judgment (see James 2:13). All along His plan has been to reconnect with us and restore what was lost in our relationship. He said, "I will meet with you and speak with you."

The revealed heart of David was to prioritize what God values and prioritizes. Again, David committed not to sleep until he dealt with the resting place for the ark...

> **"How he swore to the Lord, *and* vowed to the Mighty One of Jacob: 'Surely I will not go into the chamber of my house, or go up to the comfort of my bed; I will not give sleep to my eyes *or* slumber to my eyelids, until I find a place for the Lord, a dwelling place for the Mighty One of Jacob"** (Psalm 132:2-5).

In Bible interpretation, the Law of First Mention is applied to words used for the first time in Scripture, and is the key to its expressed meaning throughout the Word. The Hebrew word for 'ark' is first used in Genesis 50:26 in regard to Joseph's coffin.

Think of this—it's a token of man's rebellion inside the ark with a lid on it! It's a 'coffin' or representation of death. The Mercy Seat is a picture of Jesus' finished work! Do you see a glimpse of Jesus' death on the cross as the finished work in the Old Testament picture?

Place of Grace—Home

Our beloved Jesus is the center of the Church! The Lord has chosen Zion— not Sinai—a place of grace!

> **"For the LORD has chosen Zion; He has desired *it* for His dwelling place: [GRACE] 'This *is* <u>My resting place forever</u>; here I will dwell, for I have desired it. I will <u>abundantly bless her provision</u>; I will <u>satisfy her poor</u> with bread. I will also <u>clothe her priests</u> with salvation** (protection, favor)**, and her <u>saints</u> shall shout aloud for joy** (saints = holy ones, gracious ones, mercy/grace/lovingkindness)**. There I will make the horn of David grow; I will prepare a lamp for My Anointed. His enemies I will**

clothe with shame, but upon Himself His crown shall flourish" (Psalm 132:13-18, emphasis and brackets mine).

This whole psalm is based on David's devotion to God and God's promises to David. In the New Covenant, we have something even better: We have the faithfulness of Jesus and our joint-heirship with Him. The Lord was faithful to the Israelites because of David. How much more can we expect the faithfulness of the Lord because of all that Jesus has procured for us! God promised David that his seed would reign upon his throne forever, specifically speaking of Christ, and we are in Him.

Remember, the opposite of resting is working. We often so unknowingly strive in our performance. But if we renew our mind and meditate in our heart, shadow gives way to substance. All arrows point to Jesus and believing what He has accomplished through His death, burial, and resurrection. We look back upon that. He's living out His life through you and me!

Zion is the place of grace being our resting place forever. We are abundantly provided for there. We will flourish in this rest, knowing His mercy is where He meets with us and the finished work of Jesus is the central focus of our lives. This is our home.

Celebrate!

You might be wondering, "Are you suggesting that I do nothing and I'll achieve my goals?" No, of course not. Have your goals and dreams. Use your imagination. Ask yourself questions. Write down your vision or business plan. Allow the Holy Spirit to stir your heart to action. Paul said he **"labored more abundantly"** (1 Corinthians 15:10). Things will begin to fall into place for you. People and tools will begin to be attracted to you. Everything you need to fulfill this dream, vision, calling will begin to be drawn to you like a magnet. You won't have to strive. Jesus said...

"Are you weary, carrying a heavy burden? Then come to me. I will refresh your life, for I am your oasis. Simply join your life with mine. Learn my ways and you'll discover that I'm gentle, humble, easy to please. You will find refreshment and rest in me" (Matthew 11:28-29 TPT).

I've shared with you a few of my life experiences and some simple insights from the Word of God on how He brings to pass His good plans for our life. It's through resting and believing that His will emerges. In this vast expanse of freedom given to us, you can go where you're celebrated, not just where you're tolerated. So if my voice isn't being valued at the table, I'll find another table. Don't revel in religious persecution!

"If you are reproached for the name of Christ, blessed *are you,* for the Spirit of glory and of God rests upon you. On their part He is blasphemed, but on your part He is glorified" (1 Peter 4:14).

But don't allow it to be inflicted unnecessarily if you don't have to—don't adopt a persecution complex. Haven't you wasted enough time trying to appease and placate someone else that may never be willing to acknowledge your contributions? Can you completely settle in your heart not to jump through any more hoops trying to gain someone else's personal approval? If you're born again, you're already approved. Believe in and receive the only approval and acceptance that truly counts—His!

Do you realize that your inadequacies are the place where Christ can show Himself strong through you? Your weakness is His opportunity! Let that sink in...

I want to celebrate the gifts God has given me—and also yours. I will celebrate the small victories. I want to celebrate births, showers, good grades, and home ownership. I will celebrate the family and friends that I can. Travel. Eat good food. Share and serve. Laugh out loud—every day. Be kind and generous with yourself and others. Love and forgive.

Celebrate Jesus—our living Lord! Share His story with others. You have beautiful feet and are bringing the good news of His gospel of peace. Effortless change comes to us through believing the truth. And whatever we truly believe, we act upon. That's why I can say…this is *For The Rest Of Your Life*! Go ahead and live out your destiny blueprint…

It's only forever!

ABOUT THE AUTHOR

Denise Capra pioneered and founded the developing Bible College—Excel International School of Ministry—at the church she co-pastors alongside her husband, Dennis Capra—Faith Ministries Community Church in South Kansas City, Missouri. This Bible College has been compiled, packaged, and distributed all over the world. She is administrative and has a unique teaching gift and prophetic insight. Her strong mission's heart has taken her to many nations of the world. She challenges people to fulfill the internal blueprint that God has deposited in each of us. She and Dennis function side-by-side, and together have authored two books: "Dung Beetle, How to Break Free from the Performance Trap" and "Faith to the Finish". They have a few more books in the works. Dennis & Denise have two adult children, Neil and Alison.

Contact the Capra's through their websites:
www.Capramin.com
www.FaithMinistrieskc.com

Bible Versions
Copyright Acknowledgments

Sources

American Heritage Dictionary
Brown Briggs Lexicon
Foundations of Faith by Dr. James B. Richards
Heaven On Earth by Dr. Jim Richards
Leadership That Builds People Volume I by Dr. James B. Richards
Life for Today Commentary by Andrew Wommack
Living Commentary by Andrew Wommack
Strong's Concordance
Vine's Expository Dictionary
Quote by A.T. Robertson (Chapter 3)
Quote by Paul Ellis (Chapter 4)
Footnote from The Passion Translation (Chapter 4)
Quote by Joseph Prince (Chapter 6)
Quote by Dave Duell (Chapter 6)
Quote by Paul Ellis (Chapter 7)
Quote by Dr. James B. Richards (Chapter 7)
Quote by Ed Elliott (Chapter 13)
Quote by Barry Bennett (Chapter 15

Made in the USA
Columbia, SC
15 January 2020